I0793997

to linger with you

praise for *to linger with you*

"In Donna Nebenzahl's *To Linger with You*, a quest to fill a psychic void morphs into a rich family history replete with secrets and surprises. Nebenzahl's sensuous appreciation of her tropical home in British Guiana is bulwarked by careful research and a clear eyed reckoning with the legacies of slavery and indentured servitude. To Linger with You speaks of, and to, the parts of our personal heritage that don't seem to add up — and then suddenly do. This fascinating and carefully observed memoir deserves a wide readership."

— Elaine Kalman Naves, author of *Shoshanna's Story* and *Journey to Vaja*

"Donna Nebenzahl enjoyed an idyllic childhood in British Guiana, or so she thought. Her maternal grandparents, cousins, aunts and uncles had enveloped her in love. All she lacked were parents. Her eventual need for the truth about the past led her to ask a few hard questions: Why did her father die young? Why did her mother abandon her? And just who were her father's parents? Nebenzahl's discovery of the answers turns this beautiful memoir from a nostalgic evocation of Caribbean privilege into something richer, deeper and more troubling."

— Mark Abley, author of *The Organist: Fugues, Fatherhood, and a Fragile Mind*

"This is a gorgeous gift of a memoir. Donna Nebenzahl is one gifted and righteous keeper of her family stories, which are remembered and recounted here in cinematic detail. From her childhood in the home of her well-to-do grandparents, who came to what was then British Guiana from Portugal, to her life as an emigrant to Canada, Ms. Nebenzahl's family story is redolent with love and loss. *To Linger With You* can be read as a high praise song to one family and the Edenic landscape of the author's childhood home; but it is also a testament to the strength and resilience of immigrants, and a welcome and clear-eyed commentary on the many cultural influences that shaped the modern Caribbean."

— Lorna Goodison, prize-winning author of
From Harvey River: A Memoir of My Mother and Her Island

to linger with you

a memoir of sunshine and longing

donna nebenzahl

STONEHEWER BOOKS

ISBN: 978-1-0692362-2-7
eBook ISBN: 978-1-0692362-3-4

1 2 3 4 5 6 7 8 9 10

A list of permissions for quoted material can be found in the back of the book.

Cataloguing Data available from Library and Archives Canada.

Author photograph by Bruce Campbell
Set in Garamond and Futura by Emily Gaudet
Printed and bound in Canada by Friesens

Stonehewer Books | Victoria, BC
stonehewerbooks.com

Stonehewer Books is located on the traditional territory of the Lkwungen people on what is now called Vancouver Island. We acknowledge and are grateful for the unique contributions to our common well-being made by the Indigenous peoples of this land.

for George

contents

In the evening, autumn;
I think only
Of my parents

— Yosa Buson
(translated by R. H. Blyth)

prologue

I'VE BEEN DREAMING THIS STORY FOR DECADES, UNFOLDING IN MY memory the tale of a curly-haired, brown-eyed girl living in a sun-drenched paradise overloaded with colour and adventure. In my telling, this charmed upbringing revolves around a large, boisterous family, a life of comfort and security.

But there was more to the story than that. It was too easy, too sweet. While I used pretty words to describe my tropical childhood, I carefully avoided mentioning all the missing bits, the puzzle of my early life. How I resisted, clinging to the happy-family scenario: doting grandparents and flocks of aunts and uncles. I feasted on the apparent stability of my upbringing and ignored the rest.

Isn't it always so with children, who accept what they see, rarely questioning the current of uncertainty that might ripple beneath the surface? My brother George and I grew up thinking there was nothing strange about being raised by grandparents instead of parents, only glancingly aware that our father had died and knowing without understanding that our mother had made the choice to live in another country.

But if the circumstances were odd, tragic even, I didn't understand that during my childhood years. We were part of a responsible, devoted family of Portuguese who had migrated generations earlier from Madeira to South America. We lived a well-ordered life. We might have been parentless, but George and I grew up with the certainty that this was our home, these were our people. We felt special.

The first clue that I was treading on shaky ground manifested in my early teens, when I was recounting to a friend the story of my father's sudden death. I began to speak, sketching out the details as I had done over the years, when something shifted. My breath constricted in my chest, my voice tightened, and it dawned on me with a sickening shock: in that empty space I once had a father, just like everyone else did. I had a father, except he was gone. I realized it and as much as I could, being a self-centred teenager, I felt it. My father's life had ended and we had been left to carry on without him. I struggled to turn everything into a pretty story after that.

By the time I was a young woman, the murderous violence of Jim Jones and his disciples coloured everyone's perception of Guyana, the country where I grew up, which during my childhood was a colony named British Guiana. The leafy paradise of my memory was looking grim, associated now with the killings and mass suicide that took place in a remote part of the country in 1978.

In university in Canada, as I learned about slavery and racism and became aware of the cultural mix that had surrounded me during my childhood, I was disturbed by niggling feelings of shame. Growing up, I never witnessed overt belligerence or disrespect toward the descendants of the many thousands of African slaves shipped to the country to work in the sugarcane fields. Indians and Chinese had also made their way to British Guiana, suffering a longer period of indenture than my Portuguese ancestors. And while the British still ran the colony when I lived there, as they had during the time of slavery, I came to realize that all the while they had been negotiating their exit strategy.

But as a child, cloistered in this beautiful place, I was blithely unaware of the role my own Madeiran great-grandparents played. They had escaped from dire poverty and many set about constructing a life of comfort that set us apart from others, those whose skin was not white. Later, I started to feel not quite like we had been consorting with the enemy, but close.

In my middle years, another revelation. Growing up Portuguese Catholic in South America, I remember only passing references to my family name, Nebenzahl. It was certainly not Portuguese but, other than the unsupported claim that my father had been Belgian, no one in my extended family spoke of my father's story, or his ancestors. Then, after my first child was born and the birth notice appeared in the newspaper, an elderly man phoned. His last name was Nebenzahl, he said.

Was I a relative of some sort, did I have family members who came from Poland and died in the Holocaust? Not possible, I said. "I'm Portuguese Catholic. My father was born in Monte Carlo. My name is from somewhere else." It took years before I began in earnest to investigate the name and the complex story attached to it.

The Buddhist teacher Pema Chödrön reminds us that nothing ever goes away until it has taught us what we need to know. As I rummaged around in my past, the need to contemplate and tell my story, however difficult, grew more and more pressing. So I am embarking on this path, as openly and honestly as I can manage. "The most fundamental aggression to ourselves," Chödrön writes, "the most fundamental harm we can do ourselves, is to remain ignorant by not having the courage and the respect to look at ourselves honestly and gently."

This girl's life has been given so much more shape and substance than I imagined it had, recalling my early years in British Guiana. The beauty is still there, it can't be erased, but the tale is no longer only about a lost paradise. Searching has added the layers that for years I ignored or avoided. There was no trauma or cataclysmic event that hastened the process, although the deaths of my mother and stepfather, the result of slow-moving illnesses, made the path clearer to me. "Where there is strong and steady determination to move forward, a journey will quickly gather steam," advised my late friend Stephen Sims, a teacher and writer with deep spiritual understanding.

I have very little physical evidence of my life in South America. Photographs, family stories and odd bits of memorabilia have played a big part in stitching together the myriad pieces. What I do have is memory of the sights and sounds, the textures of that place that I once called home.

The cloth is still not whole, though it is more intricately worked now with the unveiling of a different family saga. The story of my last name, Nebenzahl, unfolded not in the sunny tropics but amidst the glitter of Monte Carlo and the desperate wartime streets of Paris and Marseille. I never knew this cast of characters and, except for my father, they were never to know that they made me. Here I take a few tentative steps to carve out for my ancestors, as Carl Jung suggested, answers to the questions that their lives have left behind.

part one

Go, said the bird, for the leaves were full of children,
Hidden excitedly, containing laughter.
Go, go, go, said the bird: human kind
Cannot bear very much reality.

— T.S. Eliot, "Burnt Norton," from *Four Quartets*

chapter 1

the house on brickdam street

I WASN'T BORN IN MY GRANDPARENTS' RAMBLING WHITE HOUSE IN this tiny country, a thumbprint on the northern edge of South America, but here my life began. Just days earlier, living happily in Trinidad with her young husband and baby, already expecting another, my mother had watched helplessly as he collapsed and died. She returned home, a grieving widow, delivering me into the arms of her family. I was four months old.

By the time I was three I was parentless. She had gone away, leaving my brother and me in Georgetown, the capital of British Guiana, to be cared for by our Portuguese grandparents. We remained with them until that final, life-changing move to Canada seven years later.

Our childhood memories linger in the middle range, it is said, between the ages of five and twelve. Mine glow and spark here and, maybe because of losses that I couldn't understand, I clung to home. That house was a presence in my tropical life, a sturdy sentinel as I played and dreamed through childhood. Inside, there was the comfort of its glossy mahogany floors, airy rooms and tall casement windows; outside, it stood resolute and welcoming.

I never thought to look at it straight on, study it, but I would be aware of it above me when we backed out of the carport under the house with Grandfather at the wheel of his British Vauxhall. Other times, sitting side-saddle on the back of the bicycle as Auntie Olga ferried me to and from school, I would see it looming larger as we approached, so lofty and white, the front yard filled with trees and flowering bushes and Granny's favourite potted plants, as though it had sprouted from a base of leafy foliage, from a bower of green.

Like many of the houses around us, ours was encircled. A corrugated metal wall called a paling closed off the sides, joined when it reached the garden to white picket fencing that wrapped across the front, meeting wooden gateposts and formidable double wrought-iron gates. A wide driveway flanked by low, rounded concrete parapets crossed the grass verge and open gutter that ran along the front of all the houses. These grassy roadsides were lined with trees, their wide canopies dappling the road with shade.

For me, there was no sense of danger around the place. Grandfather's security measures were common in our neighborhood: the slippery fencing was too tall to climb, and those metal gates were locked at night. I never knew, though, if our neighbours also had guard dogs like Grandfather's Alsatian and boxer, named Bruce and Rex. The dogs lived quietly during the day in room-sized cages under the house near the back steps, and I was never out at night when they did their prowling. Inside, a sweet, furry black dog named Bonzo was my childhood companion, along with various cats and the occasional caged bird.

I spent hours playing solitary games, and so I wandered, making up stories, across every inch of the paved front yard, bisected by the driveway that led to the carport. On one side, in front of the ground-level enclosed vestibule, Granny's large potted plants sprouted from black industrial drums set in a square, gravelled space: masses of waxy, heart-shaped flowers in red and white. But I always preferred the shadier part of the garden, so I played on the other side of the front yard, just behind a cascade of flowering bushes. Here, I would daydream among the pots of pink roses in Granny's tiered wooden rose arbour, or in my yellow doll's house tucked alongside a column supporting the house, near the fence.

I wasn't always alone. I would often play with my little brother, George, but mostly with my cousins Roslyn and Janis, children of my grandparents' oldest son. They literally lived next door: their home was the middle of Grandfather's three-lot property that stretched from the big white house at 46 Brickdam to a rented house on the road behind. We spent hours together, indoors and out, dark-haired girls, full of energy. All the parts of our bodies that met the sun were brown, and when we weren't in our school uniforms we ran about in light cotton dresses or shorts and sleeveless shirts. And barefoot; except for church and school, we were always barefoot.

We rarely fought, playing under the casually watchful eye of our grandparents or other family members. Though we could still be daring, at least in our own minds: standing behind the closed iron gates, we would sometimes make silly faces at passersby and at least once, after checking that no one upstairs was looking, we cheekily lifted our dresses to show our underwear. "Uh-uh, chile!" someone who spotted our daring called out, and we ran away in fright. I didn't enjoy being naughty; we were little Catholic girls with devout grandparents, so guilt came easily.

The house on Brickdam Street looked imposing — its tall, multi-paned casement windows marched across the façade, a three-sided room known as the tower punctuating one corner of the top floor. I felt calm, even happy here, but mostly I felt safe. When I looked out from the first-floor windows to the paved yard below, I could have been behind castle walls.

Sometimes my sweet-natured Uncle Charlie and his friends, all in their late teens and motorcycle-mad, would park their motorbikes inside the gates and hang about in the forecourt below, talking and tinkering. I always loved listening to conversations, and these guys really liked to banter. One day, as I leaned out the window watching them work on their bikes, a boy named Feetcow — "Dutch" was the explanation when I asked about his unusual name — spotted me and ran upstairs to give me a box of Smarties. I remember his curly brown hair, fair eyes, long face and how nice it felt to be singled out.

From those tall windows, through the canopy of trees, we could see donkey carts piled with boxes and crates trundling by on the road below, hear the hum of an occasional car, the tinkle of a bicycle bell. I could, many years later, lift from my memory the rooms of this house: the embossed fabric on my mother's pale brocade couch, a wedding gift that she left behind when she emigrated to Canada; the thin brass rod holding the stair runner that often pulled loose; the ceiling fans turning lazily. I could feel the smooth, dark surface of the mahogany dining table and the tackiness of the red-painted concrete floor in the downstairs vestibule where there was never any furniture because of the threat of the monsoon rains.

In the ten years I lived there, the first decade of my life, the house always felt stately and cool, sited in its gentility on the wide avenue, like a languid, beautiful woman in a picture hat on a street that meandered in a slow beat from the dark Demerara River all the way to the city's Botanical Gardens. For many years after I was gone, something would trigger a memory and I would be there, standing on the sparkling yellow gravel path in those gardens, or nestled in my grandmother's huge wardrobe as I explored the golden treasures in her jewelry box, the scent of her eau de cologne, 4711, saturating the air.

Later, when I had left it all behind, I would have detailed, unnerving dreams of houses. Sometimes I wandered through high-ceilinged rooms with large windows and glossy varnished floors reminiscent of the tropics. I remember gazing at brightly coloured tables and wall hangings, sun pouring in from skylights in the peaked roof. The place didn't resemble my grandparents' home, but it was tropical, I could feel it, and when I woke, I was suffused with a sense of well-being. At other, more anxious times, the houses in my dreams were shabby and decrepit, with rough wood floors and peeling paint. Once I stood on the high ground above a desolate beach, looking uneasily at an unpainted shack that sat on sand dunes I knew were shifting and unstable.

In that comfortable tropical house in Georgetown, I spent a childhood that was both privileged and empty. The story of the death of my young father just months after my birth and the departure of my mother a few years later crept into my consciousness quietly, furtively, despite the sense of family that I cultivated with such determination. In those early years, the people around me meant everything. When I did think of my mother, Gwen, on the occasion that she sent a gift or someone spoke of her, I imagined a princess or a movie star, dark-haired and red-lipped, beautiful and distant. I knew my brother and I loved her and she loved us, but even though I would light up inside when her name was mentioned, she seemed wrapped in silence.

I, who listened so carefully, was never told the story of what had happened to my father or why my mother had chosen to leave. Nor did George and I think about what would happen to us in the future. Did my relatives imagine that if they spoke about her, we would pine for her? Then what would they do? Our extended family surrounded us, made a space for us without question, and we were quite happy to play and eat and sleep. This was home, my world, the place where I stored my feelings, where my sense of loss was hidden away.

So my memories begin here, in the company of cousins and aunts and uncles and my little brother, under the quietly fierce protection of my Portuguese grandparents, who by virtue of Grandfather's determination and hard work had clambered into the monied segment of society. In that big house, we children were shielded from poverty and from the injustices of life in this country, the colony of British Guiana, known to us as B.G. For years, I had no sense of the tragedy that accompanied my own beginning nor that I was living through the difficult birth pangs of a country already tainted with the terrible usage of human beings, about to move from colonialism to a fractured new identity.

And what about our identity, we Portuguese who generations earlier had struggled across the ocean from Madeira, desperate to avoid starvation? We tried to fit in with the powerful. Granny and Grandfather had given their children names more suitable for the colonizers — my aunts were Olga, Thelma and Lucille, my mother Gwendoline — as we navigated the borders of European gentility. Gone were the names given to an earlier generation: Francisco, Jose, Leolinda.

Was our grandparents' inherited pragmatism the reason behind this? Maybe, although by the time I was growing up, our Portuguese stories and familial connections had combined with our British cultural routines to create a hybrid character. We were Guianese, at home in the tropics.

In my child's eye, the sun shone on Georgetown in the 1950s, a city of big wooden buildings, often painted white or pale yellow, with many windows. I recall the long avenues, their grass-covered medians cooled by the wide canopies of century-old plane trees, the exciting darkness of the tiny shops where we might stop to buy a bottle of lemonade, the singsong West Indian cadence of the chatty street vendor, the melodies of calypso and boisterous rhythms of the steel band. Because British Guiana was an outlier. While the colony's tongue was English — Guyana is the only English-speaking country in South America — and its body part of the South American continent, its face turned toward the Caribbean.

The thread that bound the three Guianas to the Caribbean was slavery. That foul practice that had uprooted and destroyed so many lives also brought new populations to the countries it exploited. The hundreds of thousands of Africans and Indians who settled in the three Guianas — British, French and Dutch — and the Caribbean islands were joined through similar customs, foods and that singsong lilt. Like people from various parts of so many countries around the world, the differences are there: no Jamaican sounds like a Trinidadian; no Barbadian sounds like a Guyanese. Yet so much binds them together that these four countries would establish, in 1973, the Common Market of the Caribbean.

Houses in Georgetown catch the air through slatted shutters that protect the windows. They tilt outward, deflecting the hot sun and heavy rains of the monsoon season that could, in this climate, swamp any street-level dwelling. It's not uncommon to see lizards stuck to the side of a wall or scuttling across a fence; tadpoles streaming in the gutters are a fascination for us children, especially after the rain.

Those monsoon storms terrify and amaze us. As the skies darken and the storm clouds swirl, there is a palpable feeling of moisture in the air and we children cluster, giddy with anticipation, peering out through the wide horizontal window of the L-shaped, bunk-filled bedroom we call the boys' room, on the top floor of the house.

I'm with Ros and Janis, and it feels like we're at a show, waiting with nervous excitement for the curtain to rise. We have a clear view of the sky. Below us, the outdoor back stairs lead from the kitchen to a small garden with a metal-walled privy and long-needled grapefruit tree that never bears fruit. In the distance, we hear the rumble of thunder, and we wait. The storm is approaching.

The wind picks up and suddenly the sky is illuminated, then dark again. We gasp when it's followed closely by a loud crack of thunder. The light that seems to turn the sky on and off is thrilling, but we're waiting for the awesome spectacle of that jagged flash of pure light. We know the difference between sheet lightning, when the entire sky brightens, and fork lightning — those blinding, spiky spears like an exclamation point against the dark sky. The flashing and crashing always end too quickly, then the light and the sound grow farther apart and finally the rains come pelting down, soaking the vegetation, the land, the atmosphere. The earth begins to exude that particular, delicious smell, rising to our viewing station at the window, of rainwater meeting dry ground.

It doesn't feel like we live in a wet country, though some ninety inches of rain fall on Georgetown annually. We're safe in our home and besides, we know that this is not just a weather event, it's an act of the Creator — we're witnessing the awesome power of God at play in the heavens. In my imagination, he resembles a good-natured giant rolling huge balls across the sky, though I never could figure out how he made those bright flashes. We're excited by the claps of thunder and mesmerized by the powerful, ecstatic dance of lightning that flares in the skies.

My cousins and I spent hours watching those storms, and so I was thrilled when my twelve-year-old self, now living in Canada, was able to witness a lightning storm in the skies above Prince Edward Island, at the farm guesthouse where we were on holiday. Kneeling on the Victorian settee in front of the picture window at the end of the dining room, I gazed at the fields behind us, the ocean just over the horizon, as lightning flashed across the sky. It didn't have the crackle of my childhood, maybe it was too far away, but at the same time it was scary, malevolent. The thrill vanished; I felt somehow unprotected. I don't remember ever feeling that fear in Georgetown, in my grandparents' home.

Colonialism transformed life here on the Atlantic edge of South America. The city where I grew up was buffered from the sea by the pragmatic Dutch colonizers, who in the late 1700s built a series of canals with gates that would close against the incoming tides. The British transformed the place in the early nineteenth century into a capital of tropical Victorian colonial architecture and grand avenues, cooled by the Atlantic breezes, and added a 400-kilometre-plus seawall to protect the city and parts of the coastal countryside. It was a small city in a small country, one rich with natural resources. In 1950, fewer than 60,000 people lived there; the population of the entire country was around 400,000.

But as a child, strolling with aunts and cousins along those tree-lined promenades, I was too young to realize that they were built over waterways the colonizers had created not to protect their beloved home but to keep their investment viable. I loved the wide streets, the way the tops of the tall trees shadowed the road, the ornate buildings that made the city, according to V.S. Naipaul, who visited in 1960, "the most beautiful in the West Indies." The Dutch, he suggested, gave the city its basic structure, while the British crafted the extravagant wooden buildings trimmed with fretwork and jalousied porches and the roadways whose wide grass verges on either side offered a sense of spaciousness. The city was laid out in a clear grid pattern, the north-south avenues sometimes measuring more than thirty metres across from fence to fence.

The country changed hands many times among the English, French and Dutch in the late eighteenth and early nineteenth centuries. The town, founded in 1782 during a short French occupation, was named Longchamps, established where the Atlantic met the swirling, muddy waters of the Demerara River as it flowed northward for 340 kilometres from the rainforests deep in the interior to the ocean. The French ceded control to the Dutch in 1784, who renamed the town Stabroek. When the British took over, formally at the London Convention of 1814, they honoured their king by renaming the city Georgetown. They needed the town as a central hub as they plied their lucrative trade in sugar, using slavery to do the heavy lifting.

Only much later did I learn the distressing history of the place, the blood, sweat and tears that had been shed by thousands upon thousands of people stolen — often sold by their own countrymen — from their homes in Africa and put to work in fearsome conditions in the sugarcane fields. Like any colony, B.G. was a source of revenue, whether in tobacco or sugarcane, for those who called the shots. I never asked why the people who did much of the menial labour were Black, like the servants in my grandparents' home and the porters at Grandfather's store. The language of discrimination and slavery was all around me, words used without rancour but soaked in inequality: servant, porter, plantation, coolie.

I don't recall ever seeing an Indigenous person — someone from the Arawak or Carib peoples, by then living mostly in the interior, whose home this was before the colonizers arrived. They are thought to have first used the word Guyana, meaning "land of waters." Amerindians are still about one-tenth of the population, and the most marginalized, although they are more valued now that the country is developing itself as an "ecotourism" destination.

Daily life in Georgetown was a magical mixture of many cultures. I would leave the house on an afternoon walk with my nanny, Louisa, my hair brushed into fat curls, wearing a puffy-sleeved cotton dress; then at some point I would be casually squatting in the bushes and having my bottom wiped with a leaf, a not uncommon childhood practice. This is almost the only memory I have of Louisa, other than a shadowy glimpse of someone with a wide smile and neatly curled black hair, just as I have no memory of those few early years before my mother left.

The contrasts showed up in the town itself, from Sunday mass one day, all pomp and seriousness, to the carnival procession when the Moko Jumbi, an elaborately costumed man on stilts, would walk through the streets accompanied by a steel band and a bevy of colourful dancers and peer into first-floor windows, a practice that originated in West Africa. All over the parade route, children quaked with fear in case he spotted us through the windows. As the steel drums sounded louder, meaning he was getting closer to the house, we would break under the tension and run screaming to hide under any piece of furniture that could give us shelter.

Contrasts surfaced in the foods we ate, from the refined cuppa and slice of airy angel food cake that we enjoyed during afternoon tea around my grandparents' spacious dining table to the mango dipped in salt and hot pepper that we ate on the run, scrambling down the steps of my aunts' homes in the countryside. What an explosion of taste: the delicious sweetness of the juicy peeled mango turned fiery with the dusting of salt and red pepper carried in a cupped palm.

And contrasts showed up in the music too, from the smooth American melodies of the Platters and the sonorous tones of the Latin mass to the earth-shaking, arm-swinging songs of our favourite Mighty Sparrow, a Trinidad-born calypso king, and the shimmering tunes of the steel bands playing during Carnival. Whenever that music sounded, we were on our feet and ready to dance, fancying ourselves pretty good at the Caribbean jump-up style of dancing. Both the music and the dancing, brought by Africans to these shores, were an unrecognized reminder of slavery.

◇

In those early years, my grandparents' house held me, offering space for my solitary wanderings as well as being the backdrop for the continual whirl of family life, buoyed by the energy of the aunts, uncles and cousins who filled my days with lots of loud talk, laughter, arguments, spicy food and play. Granny and Grandfather, already in their fifties, with most of their ten children married and four grandchildren living next door, were initially helped in their role as surrogate parents by my aunts Olga and Lucille. I was maybe five or six when they married young men from England and Scotland who had come to work in British Guiana.

When we weren't at school, it was usually easy to find a playmate for a game of jacks or Snakes and Ladders, or an outing with the dolls that we girls regularly dressed and undressed. We were not destructive children, but if we made a mess with our playthings, chances are we left it for one of the maids to clean up. No maid made an impression on me, maybe because these inexperienced young women never stayed around for long, likely unable to meet the standards of my grandmother, who came from peasant stock and so was even more determined to establish her gentility.

I would cringe inside, hearing the sharp voice of one of my aunts or Granny scolding someone. And decades later in Canada, when Granny met my stepfather's English mother for the first time, I stiffened with embarrassment to hear her speak of the difficulties of “keeping servants.” Nan, my step-grandmother, had spent her working life in East London as a charlady.

We could do our playacting or doll-walking everywhere in the house except in the more formal of the two sitting rooms, the one that held my mother’s wedding furniture: the cream and white brocade couch and armchairs surrounding a coffee table topped with smoked glass. I knew that this special place was linked to me somehow, although I felt no connection with its cool beauty. I rarely spent time there, an unspoken reminder of something in my past.

The focus of the other sitting room is a tall radio, nearly my height, a shining presence of varnished wood with a row of black knobs and a golden screen. Here we gather to listen to music which feels so immediate that, although I know the singers and musicians aren’t inside the radio, I’m pretty sure they’re at the radio station in Georgetown, belting out their beautiful songs. Our favourites, though, are the radio plays. We especially love *The Shadow*, a series that has run for decades, filling the airwaves with scary sound effects and ghostly voices as the adventure unfolds. I listen, mesmerized, lying on the rug in front of the radio, chin on my hands.

I loved the sleekly contoured Morris chairs and the three-seater couch in this room, covered in a pink floral fabric. Tall, quiet-spoken Innis, a delivery man at Grandfather’s store, had made the furniture and would come every year before

Christmas to refinish and polish the set. Other chairs and small tables were scattered along the casement windows that lined the front of the house, a long, narrow gallery designed for grownups. Grandfather would relax with a book there, seated on a chaise or in one of the rocking chairs by the windows.

A wide mahogany divider separated the dining room from the two sitting rooms. It held dishes and silverware behind glass doors on the upper level and, behind solid doors on the lower level, my father's books that my mother had brought back from Trinidad after his death. I, who spent so much time wandering around the house, peering into wardrobes and daydreaming, never ventured into those spaces. They spoke to me of something remote, forgotten. It felt safer to leave it that way.

At a small corner window in the dining room, we children would wait impatiently while Granny's hand-cranked vanilla ice cream hardened in its metal container. From time to time, a good-sized cage hung from the ceiling, imprisoning a colourful bird. And there were always cats, one whose puke I stepped in as I sauntered through the living room, probably because I hadn't started wearing glasses yet, and of course I was barefoot. I screeched in disgust at the thick stuff squished between my toes and screamed, "Clean my foot! Clean my foot!" to the poor housemaid.

Separated by another divider, the kitchen felt dark to me, and out of bounds because it was the cook's domain. A Dutch door above the back steps let in some light, and I recall the large stove and deep metal sink set underneath a window, and the day a huge wheel of cheese sat on the countertop. Inside, I was told, there was a large worm made entirely of cheese.

In one corner of the dining room, a staircase led to a landing on the top floor, surrounded by doors to the three bedrooms — the girls' room, the L-shaped boys' room and our grandparents' bedroom — as well as an oversized shower room. There were no bathtubs in my South American childhood; in this sultry climate, wallowing in a hot tub made no sense. The shower room was a bright kingdom where the cascading water was a mere backdrop to the games we could play. Pure white tiles covered floors and walls right up to the hinged windows that encircled the room.

Often George and I showered together, stepping over a ledge from the narrow vestibule to enter our watery playroom, full of light that bounced off those white tiles as the water rained down on them. And because the toilet was in its own little room just outside, we were never disturbed as we played in the shower; we would usually have to be retrieved by a grownup before our skin got too wrinkly. Our favourite game must have endeared us to our grandmother — washcloths in hand, water bouncing off our little bodies, we busily soaped and scrubbed the tiles.

We especially loved the sink set on the open landing, because it allowed us kids to witness Grandfather's nighttime rituals. But the unique feature on that floor lay beyond our grandparents' bedroom: the three-sided tower room where Granny and Grandfather sat every night before bed.

We often visited the tower to play or chat with our grandparents, passing through their bedroom with its twin beds and looming wardrobes. I loved climbing into Granny's tall, double-doored wardrobe so I could examine the treasures in the large jewelry box, made of pale, varnished wood, that she kept on the floor there. Nestled in, I would carefully lift the lid so the tiered shelves extended to display her precious jewelry. In many families like ours, the most prized jewelry was made from deep yellow Guyanese gold, usually twenty-four karat. Each girl child was given an embossed gold bracelet, and many matriarchs — in the tradition of their Portuguese ancestors — held a fine collection of chains, bracelets and earrings.

Granny's jewelry box contained gold and silver bangles, bracelets made of gold nuggets, heavy gold chain necklaces and many gold earrings, but I was most enamoured by one item, Granny's favourite, with the unfortunate name of "slave band." A paper-thin embossed gold bracelet, about three inches wide, it completely encircled the wrist, closed by bringing a small hole on one end over a small knob on the other. About a quarter of an inch along each edge was untouched, just shiny yellow gold, but the rest of the wide interior was filled with the most intricate gold-on-gold etchings.

There are many versions of "slave bracelets." The original, the *manilla*, a bangle made of copper or brass with knob ends, had traditionally been worn by West Africans to denote status. Eventually, though, the bracelet developed a more sinister use, as a form of currency during the time of the slave trade. After slavery and influenced by the many thousands of people who arrived in the country from India as indentured labourers, etched gold or silver bangles were favoured to adorn the wrists of little daughters. My grandmother's wide bracelet was an inspired version of those ornate, spectacular designs.

But this work of art couldn't escape its history. It made its way to Canada, still in Granny's jewel box, and after her death it was inherited by one of my cousins. At that point, the description "slave band" was considered so objectionable that she decided to melt it down and make an embossed bangle. An object of such history and beauty, never to be seen again. I still remember it on Granny's ample arm.

Our grandparents' cedar-scented wardrobes, needed because there were no closets, were so much more commanding than the pale green wardrobe in what we called the girls' room. I often slept with Auntie Olga in this airy bedroom with its mirrored vanity and double bed. But while I went to bed without complaint at night, I didn't enjoy being forced to lie down for an afternoon nap with Grandfather. He had his ritual: every day after lunch he rested, often in his own single bed or on the chaise in the tower. His snoring was legendary, he always slept on his back and we children loved to mimic the way he would relax before falling asleep by waggling his feet back and forth. We would get the giggles fanning our feet in our own beds.

One day, I grudgingly follow him upstairs to the girls' room, nestle in beside him on the big double bed, and after just a few minutes of foot-wagging, he falls into a deep sleep. But no matter how much I fan my feet back and forth, I can't drift off. I lie there bored, and then, in the interminable stillness, I become aware of life floating through those open windows — the feeling of the soft breeze upon my skin and the sounds reaching me: the clopping of a donkey's hooves down the street, the squeaking of a cart, a voice calling out to a friend or neighbour. I'm surprised to feel such sweet joy filling me up, happiness mingled somehow with longing, as though I'm a silent witness to life passing by, to a future somewhere out there. I have occasionally, in other places, other rooms, when gentle, living sounds from outside waft through an open window, been thrust back to that moment, those feelings.

Maybe because the cold grey of Montreal felt so austere, tight-lipped, just so different, I hold Georgetown in my imagination as a green and sparkling city. Within walking distance of our house, the centre of town was filled with street names of British origin: Waterloo, King, Camp, George. The two streets I remember best had distinct functions. High Street, with the public library, the law courts and many government offices, felt expansive, important. At its southern end stood a marble cenotaph, erected in 1923 to honour the Guyanese killed fighting for Britain in the First World War. It felt different from Water Street, a bustling thoroughfare that followed the contour of the river, the site of Stabroek Market with its metal and steel clock tower and bevy of small, colourful shops and a number of large department stores — among them the store Grandfather managed, known as Bettencourt's.

Closer to the Sea Wall, I recall the wide, treed boulevard where the colonial governor lived in a stately white mansion set on lush green lawns and, beyond that, the expansive grounds and long white buildings, trimmed in dark green, that housed the Georgetown Cricket Club. We often walked through the Botanical Gardens at the far end of our street, its yellow gravel paths crunching beneath our feet, brightly coloured birds trilling in the aviary.

Sometimes, on a drive with Grandfather, we would pass the town's most famous building, and even we chatty children would be silenced. St. George's Anglican Cathedral was renowned not for its flying buttresses or stained-glass windows, but because it ranked among the tallest wooden churches in the world. Standing more than forty metres high, the massive white Gothic-style church, constructed in the late 1800s, had been built of greenheart, a hardwood from the Guianese rainforest that resisted rot.

The grand cathedral awed us, but the church we knew best stood just down the road from our house. The Cathedral of the Immaculate Conception, known to us as Brickdam

Church, was a sombre Romanesque construction of reinforced concrete and granite, solidly built to withstand the tropical climate. We walked to church there every Sunday and on feast days, and I loved the cool interior and the dark wood pews, ours marked with Grandfather's name on a small brass plaque, "Frank S. Gomes and family." Even here, he was no longer Francisco.

In the late 1800s, my hometown was known as the "Garden City of the West Indies." All the main streets were planted with flowering trees, other roads with cabbage palms. Along Hatfield Street, behind our home, grew a plantation of Mora trees, tall plants that thrive in a rainforest habitat, while our street, Brickdam, featured a collection of rare tropical trees with names like "flamboyant" and "cannonball." Certain species, like the monkey-pod trees on Main Street, were able to absorb large quantities of water, important for this low-lying city. I didn't know the names of these trees, but I loved the sensation of the canopy, fluttering leaves filtering the sunlight.

But there was so much that I could not see, both literally and metaphorically. For years my weak vision went undetected, so streetlights that punctuated the road along the Sea Wall were fuzzy circles at night, and I insisted on sitting in the front row at the cinema when we went to Saturday matinees. How little I knew about the place, about what really happened, why my ancestors crossed the North Atlantic from their homes in Madeira, more than five thousand kilometres away. It took years for me to figure this stuff out, to see the foundation of exploitation, poverty and brutality upon which the entire country was built.

And we played our part. "Them cullies work hard, nuh," Granny would say, not realizing she was using the word "coolie," a name given to indentured laborers brought from India and forced to work for years before they could be free of servitude, a name almost synonymous with slave. I loved our cook — we children called her Cookie — and spoke politely to the Black maids, but I never wondered for a moment why they were relegated to a corrugated metal outhouse in the back garden, a place I would never have thought of entering. I've carried this with me, the shame of my thoughtless cruelty, the guilt.

chapter 2

a tropical childhood

EVEN THOUGH WE PLAYED TOGETHER ALL THE TIME, I WAS AWARE that my cousins had a parental connection I could never claim. George and I were tended with care by Granny and Grandfather, who were there to tuck us into bed at night and make sure we were properly dressed for school. But they weren't ours alone. And what could fill the gap in our emotional lives left by our absent parents?

I knew snippets about my mother: that she was beautiful, that she was a good student, and that she loved swimming and playing tennis. Then I learned that she had the courage to argue with her father — something my aunts would never do — because she wanted to live in Trinidad before she and my father married. I heard Olga say to her sister: "Gwen was so brave, nuh. She stood up to the old man and moved to Trinidad to be with George." He was mentioned even less, nothing beyond an occasional comment about the things he left behind or how handsome he was. The cone of silence was huge.

I can't recall her departure. The photos that show us together before she left for Canada remained the only way I could "see" us, although I've never been able to imagine what it felt like when the photo was taken. Here I am, screaming in apparent delight as my mother pushes me on a swing, children milling about at what looks like an outdoor birthday party. And look at this, the two of us posing in the photo studio, she wearing a green taffeta strapless dress and me in a little yellow dress with a frilly stand-up collar. We're both looking off camera and smiling widely, maybe at someone in the studio trying to make me laugh.

There are no photos of me holding her hand as we take a walk together, or sitting at the table near her, or snuggled up against her on the couch as she turns the pages of a storybook — simple, daily interactions between a daughter and her mother. What I've come to believe, as I look at those photographs, is that they capture special moments as a remembrance, because something significant is about to happen. My brother and I don't know it, but she is soon to leave.

Then she was gone, and I lost myself in daydreaming and in reading — comics, encyclopedias, children's novels, even newspapers — content in these worlds that grew in my imagination. "Donna, you always had your nose buried in a book," one of the aunts would later tell me. "No wonder you needed glasses, child."

I don't know how long my mother has been gone when the doll's house arrives. Maybe my parentless state triggers something in my no-nonsense Portuguese grandfather, who never plays favourites, because one day I'm busy with make-believe games in Granny's rose arbour beside the driveway when the big gates are opened and I watch, enthralled, as a dusty grey donkey pulling a creaking cart plods up the drive. Strapped to the cart, looking like it materialized out of a fairy tale, is a large wooden doll's house with a gable roof, painted a sunny yellow with white-trimmed windows and door. Matter-of-factly, Grandfather directs the delivery men to place the little structure beside the fence near the rose arbour. Had it come into the store, and he decided I should have it? Did he think I was lonely and needed something to engage my imagination? I'm entranced, then overjoyed when I realize that it's meant for me. It's mine!

Nearly every day, I make my way to the little house, bending down slightly to open the wooden door and enter. I can nearly stand up at the highest point of the roof, and all three cousins fit comfortably inside, if we crouch. Furniture is a problem we never solve; the doll's furniture I already have is too tiny, while normal furniture is too big. And even though we place a couple of small chairs inside, I often just sit cross-legged on the floor to read my book or play a game.

"Let's puh-tend!" was our favourite appeal, sung out when someone wanted to play a game of make-believe. Our pretend games were usually led by Roslyn, tall and sturdy, four years older, who could be counted on to start a game and was usually the first to overdo things and get into trouble. Both cousins wore their light brown hair shoulder-length, sometimes twirled into curls or pulled back into ponytails. The curled look was a bit babyish on Ros but suited Janis with her olive-skinned complexion and high cheekbones. Closest to me in age, she was a gentle soul who told everyone that when she grew up, she wanted to become a nun.

Our pretend games included romance, daring and rescue, and we often fought over who would play the role of the princess, convinced that it was more important to need rescuing than be the prince who did the deed. The enclosed street-level vestibule, with its dark, red-painted concrete floor, became the sea into which the hero would pretend dive — off the steps that led to the bottom landing — to rescue the princess from drowning. We were a romantic lot: the game would include lots of cries for help and heroic battling of the giant invisible waves, followed by hugs and declarations of love.

Props were always welcome, of course, so a set of brushes and mirrors on the shiny walnut dresser in the boys' room became the backdrop for saying mass, reciting our version of Latin as we solemnly placed invisible hosts on the tongues of the congregation. We could usually convince the boys to play this game, maybe because it was considered quite daring — what would Granny do if she found us pretending to be priests, much less saying mass? We girls played with dolls sometimes, dressing them up and taking them for walks, although my special doll, the one sent by my mother from Canada with movable arms and legs, her yellow-blonde hair caught in two pigtails, was too big for a toy pram. But she was the favourite of my doll students, perched on a dining-room chair, when I was playing teacher.

I shared the dollhouse too, as I knew that I should, and it added an entirely new dimension to our pretend games. Now the princess or the lady could be rescued from a burning building, or the shopkeeper could sell pencils or stones from the doorway turned shop counter. We would squat to play jacks on the wooden floor, although this was a game we could play on just about any surface, indoors or out. Sometimes we would become bakers, busy with a few metal pans lent to us by Cookie, along with a small bowl of flour and a bottle of Worcestershire sauce to wet the flour and shape it into our very special, inedible pies.

I was devoted to play, alone or with the constant group of playmates who encircled me. It filled my days and sustained me more than I realized. A child's freedom to play solitary games and experience the natural world is essential in developing an interior life, psychologists now say. This creative relationship to the world allows children to construct images of themselves and the world at large. How fortunate I was to be surrounded by such benevolence in this tropical setting.

Every Saturday afternoon before she married, Auntie Olga would take us to the movies. She felt like a companion rather than a grownup, maybe because she was still in her teens, not so far from being a child herself. My favourite aunt, she had short, cropped hair and a clear, pretty face, and she often wore pedal pushers and sleeveless blouses. She was a bit of a tomboy and could lose her temper quickly, especially when one of her many opinions was questioned.

After lunch, we would saunter along the avenues across town to the cinema. We were never late for the matinee: it was important to be early enough to see the trailers before the main feature, a habit I have never broken. We watched everything from a terrifying Dracula movie to a Ricky Nelson Western, memorable because it was the last movie I saw in Georgetown before we left for Canada. I swooned over Pat Boone as a West Point cadet and was starry-eyed watching Elizabeth Taylor and Montgomery Clift in a particularly poignant movie called *Raintree County*. We never saw any movies designed just for children — Disney movies never travelled to Georgetown in the 1950s. Nor did we ever watch television, which hadn't yet arrived in British Guiana.

Radio was our most constant entertainment. We loved radio serials and, maybe because the two aunts were still around, listened to lots and lots of music. We took songs seriously. Roslyn, Janis and I would spend hours lying on the floor with old notebooks, copying out words to the latest songs. So we decided, because we liked singing together so much, that we should become a singing group. Our first performance, planned when my mother came for her only visit back to South America, seemed a great idea at the time. We rehearsed for days, even sold tickets cut out of brown paper for five cents each. The venue was the more formal of the two living rooms, the audience occupying the long white couch and several armchairs.

All that preparation, and our girl trio should have felt ready, but as we waited on the staircase, I was suddenly beset with stage fright. What was I thinking, performing in front of this woman I hardly knew? As my mother looked on from the settee, I could feel my heart beat faster and an emptiness in the pit of my stomach, so debilitating that what should have been loud and strong came out breathless and weak. Our listeners were encouraging, but their applause was polite rather than enthusiastic.

My grandparents' bedroom at the front of the house opened onto the tower, with windows on three sides. In one corner near the entry, a small, high shelf held a statue of the Infant Jesus of Prague, wearing a golden crown, red cloak and high collar and holding an orb. But I never went in there to pray; I went to spend time with the people who sat in the two big rocking chairs that dominated that room. Every night, Grandfather would sit in his rocker, alongside the opened casement windows at the front of the room, and Granny in hers beside the other windows, facing him. This was their routine, he in his striped pyjamas, she in her nightie and dressing gown, every night before bed, rocking and talking quietly, or just sitting with their rosaries and their thoughts. In one corner stood an upright Singer sewing machine folded into its wooden shell and, piled on top, a few small pillows, zippered and tightly trimmed. Stuffed in those pillows, we were told, was Granny's long auburn hair that she cut off when she became a mother.

Before I went to bed, I would climb onto Granny's lap as she rocked slowly in the night, inhaling the sweet fragrance of the Nivea cream that she would rub on her hands, smoothing it gently on her fine, mottled skin. She had small hands with strong, blunt fingers and short nails. No-nonsense hands. I would sometimes trace the veins under her soft skin and feel the bumps around the knuckles, thickened with arthritis. She would massage her fingers occasionally, but her knees hurt the most. She was not yet sixty and quite round, and would often sit and rub her swollen knees in a circular motion, complaining quietly.

As we sat rocking in the tender night and I snuggled on her lap, Granny would tell me stories. But these weren't pretty bedtime tales about princesses and golden eggs; they were disturbing stories about obeah, what people used to call black magic. Despite her reach for gentility and her devout Catholicism, something in these elemental, even violent stories spoke to Granny, whispers from the heart of this tropical country. They were macabre and unnerving — as they were meant to be — a mixture of African folklore and jungle tales. Even though we're of Portuguese stock, Granny seemed to be saying, these stories are part of our folklore too. I took the same scary satisfaction from them as she did.

One of Granny's favourites was the story of the tailor who became suspicious when his wife kept leaving the house at night.

"I can't sleep, I'm going to take a walk," she told him. But it happened so often that one night he followed her and found her in a clearing in the woods, dancing naked around a bonfire with a group of similarly undressed people. They were practising a satanic ritual! The tailor was horrified and angry, so he decided to make a point. He took out his tailor's needle and poked one of the cavorting men in the butt, retreating into the darkness so he wouldn't be seen. That person blamed the one beside him, and so on, and soon enough everyone was yelling and fighting. This was a weird, funny story, and Granny would chortle as she described the naked men and women in the flickering firelight, leaping and running about.

Her scariest story was the cautionary tale about the woman from a small village on the edge of the jungle who decided one day to make jam. Donning a pair of heavy black boots, she went out to pick berries for her jam, even though she was always being warned, Granny said, not to venture into the jungle. In pursuit of that luscious fruit, the woman got too close to the trees arching over the forest floor, home of many wild creatures including the mighty boa constrictor, whose method of killing was to drop down on prey and squeeze the life out of them. When night was falling and she hadn't returned, her worried family went looking and discovered, to their horror, a huge boa constrictor stretched out to its full length, digesting, a human-sized lump inside its body. They knew it was the berry picker because, despite its ability to unhinge its jaws and swallow its prey whole, the snake was unable to ingest those large black boots. There they were, sticking out of its mouth.

We didn't anger our grandparents often, so it felt catastrophic when we managed to upset them. The Grey Ghosts were one of those miscalculations. We were so mesmerized by the Classics comic about the girls in an English boarding school who threw on grey cloaks at night to solve mysteries that Ros, Janis and I decided to follow their example. Who knew the mysteries we could solve?

We spent a few days secretly stitching together our own "cloaks" out of scrap material and carefully deposited them in the drawer in the girls' room wardrobe. That night, we organized it so they could sleep over with me in the double bunks of the boys' room, while George was staying next door. Mystery-solving time. We stayed awake until the house settled and we could only hear our grandparents murmuring in the tower. Then, on tiptoes, we, the tropical Grey Ghosts, crept across the landing to retrieve our cloaks. Slowly, slowly we pulled open the big drawer.

Unfortunately for us, Grandfather heard the noise and, because the tower and girls' room windows were across from each other, he thought someone was eavesdropping. "Who's there?" he yelled, and he leapt from his rocker to investigate. In terror, we abandoned our cloaks and raced back across the landing to dive back into our bunks — except, like the kid left without a chair during a game of musical chairs, I didn't make it to my bed. By the time Grandfather arrived, there I was, quivering in Janis's bed.

It took some quick talking to explain to him the work of the Grey Ghosts, secretly solving mysteries in the night like the girls in that boarding school in England. He was not impressed. The cloaks were never retrieved again from the wardrobe drawer, and I did find out something about privacy and the invisible boundaries that children sometimes cross.

As it turned out, my sweet, doting grandmother was much more formidable when angry. I learned this because of a drink that George and I loved, called Rainbow Chocolate Milk. It came in a box, a powder that magically transformed a glass of milk into chocolatey deliciousness and, unfortunately, was the only weapon at hand one afternoon when my brother started teasing me. He was halfway down the outside back steps from the kitchen and I was looking out the Dutch door when the taunting began. As I stood at the top of the stairs with a glass in my hand, my fury spilled over. I just had to shut him up, so as he turned to look at me, I flung the milk from my glass at him, my precious Rainbow Chocolate Milk. And it worked! He was sopping and now, instead of teasing me, he was crying, wailing. "I can't see, I can't see! I'm blind!"

Of course he wasn't, only shocked and somewhat chocolate-milky, but I knew immediately that I was in trouble and bolted upstairs to the girls' room. I knelt beside the big bed and began to pray: "Oh my God, I am heartily sorry …" I murmured, my heart beating hard with fear. But that wasn't enough for Granny. Perhaps she was frightened that I had really hurt George, or perhaps she was upset that I had wasted food, literally spilled milk, and what about the starving children in Africa? She found me there, kneeling and praying, but that didn't soften her heart.

She slapped me, not hard enough to hurt but definitely to scare. Much worse than that, she told me I would be sent to an orphanage. What possessed her to say the most terrible thing to a child who had no parents? I got into the shower full of tears, my wailing and runny nose lessening as I stood under the cascading water. By the time I got into my pyjamas I was sniffling, which is how Grandfather saw me when I was called down to the table for tea.

Granny recounted the story quietly and I knew the storm had passed. "I'm sorry," I said again, and Grandfather only looked at me. Perhaps, especially since George was sitting at the table with perfectly functioning eyes, he knew that Granny had gone too far. It was a cozy feeling, after a good cry and a shower, safe at home, having tea and cake.

My brother was born six months after our father died, and was given his names, George Louis Paul. I was only a few months old when my mother conceived again; did my father have a premonition that his time was running out? My brother was one of those beautiful boys, and when we posed for our annual formal studio portrait to send to our mother, with his dark hair carefully parted on the side and brushed off his forehead, his gold-flecked hazel eyes, his little white suit, shirt and tie, George was the proverbial "handsome little man." We were both self-conscious, but he looked gravely at the camera in those photographs, while I tended to pull faces and grin.

I looked at my brother through a child's eyes, which usually meant as a playmate. I had no clue whether he understood what it meant to be parentless. Granny loved him, doted on him really, but I don't think he was as close to Grandfather, who had a somewhat distant relationship with his own sons. George was a busy child, playing with his cousins or tinkering with a toy, always part of some game or activity. But while he played and rough-housed the way little boys did, my brother also hurt easily. "Granfaddah, Roslyn hit me!" was one of his refrains when his larger girl cousin settled some dust-up with a slap.

Then when George was about five years old, he developed "kidney troubles," a simple way of describing nephritis, when the tissues of the kidney become inflamed and have trouble filtering waste. There must have been some danger to his health — the condition can result in kidney failure — because he was hospitalized for a time. He didn't look sick when my cousins and I visited him in the hospital, but I remember him sitting there, at the end of a long white room with beds arrayed on either side, near large windows opening onto a wide terrace. And even though we played happily on his bed with some of the many toys he had there, he looked so small and quiet when our visit was over and we walked away. After he came home, I never thought to ask him how it felt to be left in that big hospital at night, when he was all alone.

Granny visited him often; I'm sure she told him how much she prayed to the Blessed Virgin to make him well again. Grandfather, I imagine, would have said something like "Buck up, boy." But we children weren't worried about George. We knew that Granny had previously achieved a miracle when one of her sons, Stanley, had been in a coma when he was young. She prayed and Uncle Stanley recovered, so naturally we reasoned that George was going to be just fine. I never considered that her magical powers hadn't extended to saving my father.

My brother returned home after a few weeks, and during the day slept in one of the twin beds in Granny's bedroom. He must have been too weak to walk — I can remember her carrying him piggyback to the bathroom. She used all her wiles with native remedies to help him; I recall her picking him up from her bed and placing him gently in a large metal tub full of steaming water and floating green leaves. He lost an entire year of school to the illness, and that was when my mother came back to British Guiana for her only visit during my childhood. What sticks is that I was perturbed because my brother got so much attention. I never appreciated how serious his illness was — I only remember that he got the lion's share of toys that Christmas.

The year when he was out of school, being nursed by grownups, put a distance between us. We might have looked alike, slender children with dark hair and bunny teeth, but I always felt so much older than him. We grew up together, but there was so much we never talked about. George became a skilled photographer and cabinetmaker, and while I never heard him describe his childhood as unhappy, he had experiences that would have shaken up any child. During most of them I was a bystander, immersed in my own world of books and play.

Like me, George was surrounded by aunts and uncles and cousins — Paul was some four years older and Andrew was near his age. He was an inquisitive kid, but his curiosity suffered because, for my brother, going to school was a nightmare. Maybe it was my grandparents' desire to give a little girl more protection that informed their decision to send me to a convent school with schoolbooks and kind teachers, while my brother, with his occasional stutter, was sent to Brickdam School, the public school just down the street.

I saw it only from the outside, a brown-painted wooden building with a long verandah and boisterous, noisy children spilling out of classroom doors. Unlike me with my notebooks and stars, these students did their work on slates, and teachers routinely hit them. I visualize mayhem when I think of that school, so why was my little brother sent there to fend for himself?

No wonder he decided to opt out. Instead of walking to school one morning, he hid in a large room under the house where old furniture was stored. He must have been down there for a few days, making his way upstairs for lunch, pretending the entire time that he was just back from school. How sad and scary that would have been! I was oblivious to his hiding away — so much for my investigative skills — and I can imagine how lonely he must have been in that dark room. Did Cookie figure it out and tell Granny, or did the school finally decide to check on his absence?

I had just returned from my own school when I saw them clustered in the room where he had been hiding: a school official, my grandparents and my frightened little brother. Although I can't recall a punishment, it was enough that he was sent back to the school. George was a creative, engaged kid who loved knowing how things work, but he never looked forward to going to school the way I did.

Granny's big mahogany dining table, an expanse of glossy dark wood with smooth bevelled edges surrounded by eight wooden chairs with curved backs, was the heart of the house. This is where my brother and I and our grandparents, joined sometimes by one or two cousins, aunts or uncles, gathered each day for breakfast, lunch, tea and dinner. But the room was empty between mealtimes, and those chairs occasionally became part of my solitary game of teacher. I would line up the chairs in rows of two, my chair facing the "class," carefully place a used school workbook on each chair, sometimes a sitting doll, and then proceed to pick up and correct the "work," just like I saw my teacher do.

The only player of this game, I nevertheless conversed with my invisible students, reprimanding some and praising others by writing a crisp V.G. on the page, meaning "very good," occasionally pasting on a gold star from my stash. I had quite a few of those, because at my real school I sat studiously at the front of the class, the only place where I could see the board, and so accidentally became a good student. I don't remember the lessons seeming hard, or being told to study, I just did the work. I was an overachiever because I had no sense of what was expected of me.

I came first in my class in one of those early grades, and when Granny saw my report card, she was overjoyed, lifting me up and hugging me, beaming with pride. She was rarely given to such expressions of happiness, so I was happy too. But mainly I was anxious about how I was going to find my place in the assembly hall when the students of each class were called out by order of achievement, a tradition at school after the reports were sent home. (Did the poor kid who came last get singled out just like I was? I never thought to check what was going on behind me.) The teacher took the class there and showed me a mark on the floor where I would go first, and then the other students would follow. My heart contracted when I realized that by the time we went back to the spot from which we would be called, I couldn't see the mark any longer. I fumbled my way through the ceremony. Nobody, including me, had yet realized that I was severely short-sighted.

That wasn't the only clue that I couldn't see well. Standing with my cousins one day, looking out the window of the girls' room, I searched vainly as they busily described a scene on the street below. "Look, see the man, nuh?" one told the other. "Why he walkin' his bike?" Try as I might, I couldn't see this man walking down the road, but I was silent, pretending rather than revealing my fuzzy vision. It was thanks to my mother's observation — was she looking at me more keenly, not having seen me for so long? — that I was sent to the optometrist.

That first pair of glasses changed my life. I walked out into a new world, seeing definition all around me — shopfronts, flowers, words on a billboard. When we went for an evening drive, the streetlamps were no longer fuzzy but defined spheres of light. I hadn't known what I was missing, and so, what a revelation! Still, because I had come to enjoy looking at the world close up, which I could still do without my glasses, I continued to sit at the front of the class and to peer closely at my picture books.

Although I was surrounded by family, I did venture out, tentatively. Sometimes I would cross the road to another big white house with cool, dark floors, the home of one of my few friends, a quiet Chinese girl named Helen with sleek dark hair and a shy, sweet smile. We were close enough friends that I invited her to the only tea party I ever hosted, in the downstairs room under the house, the same spot where George had hidden. It was a storeroom with lots of dark corners, but Granny pulled out a low wooden table that she helped me set with a lacy white cloth. As we teetered on mismatched chairs, I carefully poured tea into the ornate gold-trimmed demitasse cups that Granny never used because we never drank coffee. We children all drank tea, weak with milk and sugar.

I would sometimes head off in another direction with Roslyn, who was friends with the daughter of our family doctor. Dr. Ramdehal's big house was set apart because it contained a large concrete swimming pool. It was above ground, so you had to climb a ladder to get in. I never ventured in there, imagining slimy concrete walls and who knows what at the bottom. Dr. Ramdehal always seemed to be on call for us, since Roslyn had a penchant for falling off bikes and received all manner of scrapes and bruises. Slightly overweight, always cheerful, he was utterly dependable whether he was bandaging a twisted ankle or delivering a baby.

I was comfortable and happy at my school, the Ursuline convent. The large wooden building resembled a cloister with covered walkways created by the extended second floor encircling a grassy central courtyard. The Ursuline nuns had arrived in Georgetown in 1847, six young nuns from Athlone, Ireland, and the order ran schools there until they were taken over by the government in 1976. These women looked and sounded different from us. It wasn't just their wimple and gown; their skin was very pale, and they spoke without the singsong West Indian lilt. They were organized without being punitive, walking among us with serenity, and so I felt unthreatened. I found them neither tremendously holy nor particularly strict, although being such an obedient child, I would never have incurred anyone's wrath.

The way people behaved at school fascinated me. I looked longingly at the high-school girls, who wore white blouses under dark blue V-necked uniforms with lightly pleated skirts, so much more serious than my uniform, a blue and white gingham dress with puffy sleeves and a Peter Pan collar. I tried to copy the way the Mother Superior's hands, placed together during the daily prayer, would be slightly cupped, or how one of the teachers would thrust her hand inside her blouse to straighten her bra strap. I wore an undershirt and found that movement compelling.

When we weren't in class, students could go into the quadrangle for short recesses. Groups of older girls from the adjoining St. Rose's High School walked by, engrossed in what looked like important conversation. I couldn't imagine what they were talking about but longed to be so engaged in a discussion. Mostly quiet myself, I recall the chatter, at the end of each school day, as I sat with other students on the sweeping staircase at the front of the school, waiting to be picked up to go home.

I was secure here, despite the anxiety of finding my place on the assembly floor at the end of term, and the scary sweetness of performing on stage at a school concert. It was a small part, one of the bluebells in Tchaikovsky's "Waltz of the Flowers," but I treasured the powder-blue papier mâché skirt that curved upward like opened petals and the little blue petal hat with its green stem. An uncomplicated dance, a little swaying from side to side, a bit of twirling — but I felt like I had entered a magical kingdom of dancing blooms and fairy princesses.

I memorized the words of many of the songs I heard on the radio, entranced by the poetry and the rhythm. Most afternoons, after being brought home from school, I would rush upstairs, drop my books, pull off my school dress and proceed downstairs in my matching blue-and-white gingham underpants and white undershirt. I was in a hurry because I needed to get to that beautiful upright piano in the corner of the living room where I would spend the next few hours perched on the piano bench, plunking away at the keys. This is one of the few memories where my pleasure was tainted because Grandfather once scolded me when he came home. Instead of praising my skill at playing Chopsticks, he said, "Donna, don't let me catch you round here in your underwear."

On the weekend — and sometimes after a weekday supper if the evening was especially steamy — we children would climb into Grandfather's little Vauxhall, with the signal flag that poked out from each side when he was making a turn, and go for a drive. My favourite vantage point was standing in the back, just behind Grandfather's head, resting my hand on the cross-hatched skin of his sun-browned neck. Sometimes he drove slowly on the road that bordered the Sea Wall, a flat-topped construction of concrete and stone that protected the city, which was below sea level, from the Atlantic Ocean.

Built mostly by convict labour in the mid-1800s, it replaced a series of earlier walls ruined by heavy rains and high tides. An engineering marvel, the wall stretched and curved, hugging the coastline for more than 450 kilometres. And it served its purpose: in conjunction with dykes and the many canals that traversed Georgetown, it managed, despite the occasional breach, to keep the city from being inundated during the monsoon season.

But there was no ocean when I was growing up, only dried mud as far as the eye could see. We were allowed once or twice to climb over the Sea Wall and walk along the cracked muddy surface on the other side, easily reached because the concrete and brick supports that faced the sea were built on a gentle slant. I walked gingerly, too afraid to venture far out, imagining the cracked mud might split apart and I would fall into a crevasse of deep, dank water. That period of dry seabed must have lasted only during my childhood; floods in later years continued to break through various parts of the wall.

One day along that same seawall, Uncle Charlie's friend Feetcow was riding his motorcycle when a cow wandered onto the road. He tried to avoid the animal, lost control of the bike, and was fatally injured. So when I got home from school, perhaps needing company because Grandfather was at work, Granny appeared at the door of the girls' room just as I had pulled off my school dress, saying, "Come, child." There was an urgency in her manner that was new to me. I hurriedly put my dress back on and followed her down to the waiting car, not realizing I would be making my first visit to a funeral home. The room we entered felt dark, crowded with strangers, and at that point I lost track of Granny, Uncle Charlie, everybody. I was fixated by the sight that appeared through the milling crowd: a woman stood there weeping, her son's body laid out beside her in a dark wood coffin.

Sundays. We are not allowed to eat before going to mass, a ritual of such importance that no one tries to get out of it or sneaks into the kitchen to grab a slice of bread. We girls are in our Sunday best: decorous flowered dresses, white ankle socks, hats that tie under the chin and purses that we carry daintily on one wrist. The boys, like Grandfather, wear suits and ties. Our grandparents take this seriously, but sitting through mass isn't easy. Not only are we hungry, but once we're through kneeling and standing and are forced to sit through the readings and sermon, we start to fidget and poke at each other. Until Grandfather notices. A few sidelong glances, then he leans over to place a large hand on a jiggling knee. There's no fear that he will hurt us, but once he makes it clear that he's displeased, we are shut down.

After mass comes my favourite moment: Sunday breakfast. We sit together around the table, the feeling of having sacrificed for this reward making it that much sweeter. Cookie's beef stew is a Sunday morning favourite. In front of me, a plate swimming with dark, thick broth studded with bits of beef, carrots and potatoes. There are others around the table but I'm in a dream world, eating slowly, a feeling of well-being running through my body. I butter a slice of bread which I tear into ragged squares and place around the plate to soak up the broth. Then, one by one, with my fork, I scoop up those stew-laden bread bits and pop them in my mouth, each bite a savoury explosion of flavour.

Sometimes our Sunday drive along the Sea Wall includes a visit to a spot called Dixie, with a beautiful bandstand set in an open field, the sea just beyond the bluff. A favourite stop when the weather is fine, crowds gather here on Easter Sunday, which marks the beginning of the kite-flying season.

On this day, dozens of kites are dancing in the breeze. Like most Guyanese children, we take this play seriously, combining as it does the energy to run and launch the kite and the skill to manipulate the string and keep it in the air. Nothing is more important than keeping your kite aloft, soaring and dipping in the breeze. We are kite-crazy, joining the swell of children laughing and yelling, each one holding on to a kite and string.

I run across the open ground, bubbling with excitement. Then, when I feel the pull of the wind, I throw my hands up in the air to launch my kite. My goal is to keep running, running, tugging on the loosening string with long sweeps of my arm to help it climb and climb. The moment I feel that the kite is up there, I stop, turn to face the kite and tug with shorter, tighter movements to keep it aloft. I almost always succeed, although no one in our family has the kite skills of my cousin Paul, who can make his kite swoop and soar. The sky is crowded with kites in blue and yellow and green, triangular kites with long, beribboned tails and box kites with a different colour on each panel. But it doesn't matter if your kite is made of newspaper glued to sticks with ragged pieces of cloth for a tail — as long as it flies. Hours of kite flying leave us breathless and exhilarated.

Some Sunday afternoons, we take a stroll through the Botanical Gardens and zoo. Nearly two hundred acres dug out of swampy pastureland, the gardens were begun in 1877, a wondrous place with rows of stately palms and riotous greenery, bird calls and animal sounds. Mostly I remember the zoo: huge snakes in cages, the boa constrictors of Granny's nighttime stories, their fat, exquisitely marked bodies curled and folded. Brilliant peacocks saunter about, their trailing feathers occasionally bursting into shimmering emerald fans. I am enraptured, mostly, by the slippery, lazy manatees who live in the gardens' two lakes, each traversed by nineteenth-century curved iron "kissing" bridges.

The manatees, whose ancestors were brought here when the zoo opened, sometimes surface out of the dark water, peer out, then just as slowly slip back into the murky depths. I like their sweet, good nature, their soft eyes. Yet maybe because the lake, bordered with water lilies, is almost level with the dark green grass surrounding it, I always feel a certain anxiety as I peer into the depths trying to figure out how, if I fell in there somehow and a manatee saved me — as I knew it would — I would be able to hang on to such a slick body.

I can recall walking with my nanny, Louisa, hearing the crunch of the fine yellow gravel along the garden paths — meaning I must have been about three years old and my mother might have still been in Georgetown, back at the house with my little brother. How lovely to imagine that. I am captivated by those paths and how the dips in the yellow gravel hold the water that spills around the outdoor water fountains, simple metal and stone contraptions with a small step for children. I lean down, fascinated, to ponder those tiny pools of water, glittering on the gravel which rises around them like miniature mountains and valleys, creating magical little kingdoms on the path.

One Sunday, on our way to the gardens, we turn right beyond the racetrack and begin to drive along dusty roads bordered by a warren of simple dwellings. We stop outside a little wooden house and only then do I realize that we're paying a visit to Cookie. Was it insulting that I only knew her as a function until I was an adult, long departed from B.G.? Or was it just a childish thing, my ignoring or erasing her name? The aunts knew better. "She named Cookie Charlotte," Auntie Olga told me. "We always called her that."

Cookie was a staple in my life. A solidly built, good-natured woman with a large, round face, she always wore a faded floral apron and old shoes with flattened backs that let her heels breathe free. I'm sure she would have preferred to be barefoot. We loved her not just for her wonderful cooking but for her cheery disposition.

She lived in a part of Georgetown I had never seen before, so there must have been a reason for our visit. Was she not well and had Granny sent her something? Had she made something special for us that we were picking up? We children hung by the door and peered into Cookie's little house with its few furnishings. It seemed an unnerving setting for someone we saw daily in our large kitchen, someone who was so much a part of our life there that it felt unnatural she would be anywhere else. We greeted her shyly.

Did her home have a dirt floor, I remember wondering later. I am ashamed to think it did, and she came to work every day, full of love and kindness, to our fine house with its polished floors. I'm even more troubled to remember that throughout my childhood she addressed my brother and me as "Master George" and "Miss Donna."

Maybe Georgetown felt so easygoing because we moved about not hearing the roar of cars but the ringing of bicycle bells. Here, folks biked to see friends, biked to work, biked to the bustling Stabroek Market, biked to the tennis courts or the cricket fields. Like many schoolchildren, I hoisted myself onto the flat seat behind the rider nearly every school day. Sometimes Auntie Olga but most often Manu, Sonny or Innis, one of the deliverymen from Grandfather's store, would ferry me as I perched sidesaddle on the back of the bike. To school, home for lunch and back again, until the final pickup at the end of the day from the school steps, where I sat waiting with the other children.

As a child I thought of them like family, those men, all descendants of the slaves brought to the country to harvest sugarcane. I saw but didn't see that they were Black. So were all the people at work on my grandparents' property except for the Indian gardener, whose ornate silver ankle bracelets tinkled as she busily sprayed DDT around the deep corners of the garden.

In the colonial life in which my family participated, the British were in charge. The governor in his fine mansion represented the Queen, the lady with the crown who was the head of our Commonwealth. I didn't see the structures of class and race or realize at the time that our overlords were about to relieve themselves of their colonial tenure. Our life was marked by a casual racism toward the Black population, who lived mostly in simple circumstances, and were considered not capable of achieving a lot. Much later I wondered why the British, knowing they were going to exit, didn't do more to prepare those who would replace them.

The Portuguese, Chinese and Indians who had come as indentured labourers didn't have to deal with the cruel sweep of slavery, but being indentured meant that they spent their first few years in the country indebted to the British plantation owners who brought them here to replace the slaves. More than 30,000 Portuguese arrived between 1835 and 1882 — the first indentured workers brought to the country. Until they paid off the cost of that indenture, they had to deal with miserable working conditions, and although most of them were seasoned agricultural workers, they quit the plantations as soon as they could.

The British needed more workers and found them mainly in India. Lured mostly under false pretenses, they did not arrive in chains but were in bondage nevertheless. Intimidated, coerced, even kidnapped, they were free only after five years' work on the plantations. Mostly Hindus, from small villages in North India, they belonged to many different castes and their forced mingling had one positive effect: it muddied the traditional hierarchy, often benefitting people in the lowest caste who were able to discard the shackles of that exclusionary system. Between 1838 and 1917, at least five hundred ships transported more than 200,000 indentured Indian immigrants to British Guiana. The majority made a go of it, marrying and intermarrying. By 1917, Indo-Guyanese were the largest ethnic group in the country, making up more than forty per cent of the population.

Yet even though the system of indenture muted the traditional hierarchies of caste that existed it India, it was anything but benevolent. These labourers, including children, worked in the cane fields more than twelve hours each day, suffering abuse at the hands of overseers and managers. They were paid meagre wages and faced working conditions so onerous that many died. Even after they had worked five years and could either return to their home country or stay on, they lived with the stigma of their servitude and poverty. Despite occasional riots and concern by some members of the British establishment — the Colonial Secretary Lord Russell in 1840 described the situation as a "new form of slavery" — the need to build a new life won out.

The ancestors of Manu, Sonny and Innis had arrived in the 1660s as slaves from Africa, brought by the Dutch colonizers to perform backbreaking work in the tobacco and sugar plantations. For two centuries they struggled in brutal conditions, overworked, undernourished, often punished cruelly for any perceived transgression. Even in freedom, with little education or opportunity, they continued to struggle. In my grandfather's store, the men who worked as porters fetched and carried for little pay.

But their lives were intertwined with ours, not only because they could be depended on to deliver me to and from school, but because of their skills as healers and craftsmen. Maybe, if they were white, they could have made a living in medicine or carpentry, but here they were deliverymen with special powers.

Sonny McLeod was the one I knew best. A medium-sized man with a round face and easy smile, a thinning crop of curly hair and a small moustache, he was unerringly kind and good-humoured. I trusted him completely and so did Granny, who called on Sonny one day after I had developed a deep ache in my stomach. She was sure this was the result of jumping off the side of the back steps that led from the Dutch door outside the kitchen — "How many times I tell you, chile, not to do that? It make you sick, nuh?" That this game of chicken never resulted in broken bones is a wonder; we basically dared each other to jump from a higher and higher step down to the ground until someone didn't have the nerve to go any higher. Granny believed the reason for my aching belly was that my stomach couldn't take all that jumping and had "dropped."

So Sonny, who had experience with these sorts of things, came to the house to administer to me for this condition, known as "narrah," which apparently meant any pain in and around the belly. I lay on Granny's bed, tummy exposed, and he crouched over me and gently rubbed some sweet-smelling salve on my stomach, massaging my belly with a firm, gentle circular motion, smiling all the while. I closed my eyes. My stomach ache went away.

I found Manu very handsome. Tall and quite bald, he didn't perform any healing rituals on me, but he knew how to cheer up a hot little girl after a busy day at school. Ferrying me home on the back of the bike, he would sometimes stop when we saw the street vendor whose cart held a huge block of ice and assorted bottles of coloured syrups. Once I had chosen a particular fruity flavour, the man would shave ice into a paper cup and slather it with syrup, which I would quickly eat with a small wooden spoon. Or we might come upon the guy selling channa from an outdoor brazier — chickpeas roasted with a touch of salt and hot pepper, unforgettably spicy and served in a paper cone.

Both Manu and Innis, an older, quieter man with a solemn face and kind eyes, were skilful carpenters. Innis made the high, deep mahogany sideboard with sliding glass doors that divided the living and dining rooms in my grandparents' house, repository of my mother's wedding silver, which Cookie polished each week, and my father's books. I was mesmerized by the cabinet that Manu had made to hold Grandfather's liquor collection, a glass-sided, mirror-bottomed portable bar on wheels, made of various types of exotic wood. When the two doors at the top were lifted open, the interior mirrored tray would rise, bringing up the bottles and glasses. It was solid and purposeful, yet it sparkled and tinkled. I thought this the most beautiful piece of furniture I had ever seen.

We ate all our meals around that expansive dining table. Though I never heard her speak about being proud of her cooking, Cookie was always smiling when she proceeded from the kitchen, her domain, carrying fragrant platters or tureens of cook-up rice and beans, noodles and stews. She was always busy, and although we knew better than to hang around underfoot, Cookie could be prevailed upon to spend a moment with a little child who needed a hug. I remember the warm smell of her body, the roughness of her hands.

Into my small world, Cookie delivered one of its greatest pleasures. She was responsible for the variety of flavour that was our cuisine, a mixture of Indigenous, African, Caribbean and Portuguese, with a lot of Indian and a little Chinese thrown in for good measure. Her curries were a staple though her stews were the most popular, made from what we would now call castoff cuts of meat, cooked slowly for so many hours that the tender morsels nearly fell apart. How else would you eat pork hocks and oxtail? When I knew more about cuts of meat, I wondered if the English got the steaks and roasts which were never part of our diet, or whether Cookie simply prepared the meats she knew best.

Didn't matter; we loved it all, or almost all. My taste buds rebelled at souse: even its name resembles something hidden and slimy, a broth made of pickled pig's feet with onion, garlic and lime. It couldn't be saved even by a generous addition of hot Scotch bonnet peppers.

But how to describe the mouth-watering, pungent flavour of pepperpot, a dish with Indigenous antecedents based on casareep, a dark, thick syrup taken from the cassava root, reputed to keep meat from spoiling? The most popular dish in British Guiana, its flavour was unrivalled — a nearly black broth in which chunks of meat, like beef, lamb, pork or goat, and sometimes pigs' trotters, had been simmering for hours. It wasn't pretty. What you saw was steaming dark liquid on which sat a chunk of fatty meat, still on the bone. The revelation came when that piece was cut open and the fat fell away. That perfectly tender meat inside was so delicious, the broth so intense, the flavour both sweet and smoky, that I had to close my eyes for a moment. With buttered bread, we would eat pepperpot at lunch, dinner or sometimes, wonderfully, breakfast.

We gathered every day for lunch, including Grandfather, who would sit with us over a leisurely meal, then rest before returning in mid-afternoon to Bettencourt's. We always celebrated when Cookie made metemgee, another childhood delight, a concoction of root vegetables cooked in a broth of coconut milk. I would slather the thick coconut sauce over the yams, eddoes and plantain and mash them all together, savouring the fragrant, earthy flavour. Other times Cookie would make chow mein, a West Indian variety without bean sprouts. She brought it to the table on a platter, a huge mound of flat egg noodles loaded with vegetables and sliced, hard-boiled eggs.

I enjoyed black pudding, a fat sausage filled with rice mixed with black, congealed blood and many spices, served sliced and best eaten without thinking too hard about its contents. And I looked forward to delectable salt fish, another stew, this one with shreds of long-soaked salt cod, soft rounds of onion and slices of hard-boiled egg in a buttery broth. Sometimes at lunch, Cookie would bring a jug of lemonade to the table or my favourite, sorrel, a clear red drink with an unforgettable herbal sweetness made by soaking sorrel, a tropical hibiscus flower, in water with ginger, orange peel and cinnamon sticks.

It would then be strained and sweetened and served in an ice-filled glass.

Granny, on the other hand, always favoured more healthy foods, except for special occasions when she would make ice cream in a large metal churn. We loved to watch as the interior well, surrounded by tightly packed ice and rock salt, filled up with thick milk and vanilla. Then the lid would be screwed on and Granny, with a little help from us children, would turn the crank until she deemed the ice cream ready. No ice cream has ever compared to the creamy, vanilla-studded mixture we ate in little white bowls.

But most of the time, she savoured dishes like callaloo soup, a broth of African ancestry made from the green leaves of the amaranth plant, slightly bitter and nutty. For breakfast every morning, she would eat half a papaya, claiming the dark orange flesh inside the long, squash-like fruit offered the great benefit of regularity. Maybe Granny was right; she lived, in relatively good health, until the age of ninety-two.

She did go overboard sometimes with the internal cleansing, however. Once a month, we were told to line up to have our intestines cleansed with a dose of castor oil, its flavour and smell so disgusting that I would retch when the spoon got close. But the other cleanse, the one brought out only when the need arose, was much, much worse. I recall kicking and screaming as I tried to escape from the enema, needed apparently because I was constipated and Granny always kept track.

I never succeeded; while someone held up the metal canister filled with soapy water, Granny inserted that nasty tube up my bum. She believed in scouring the system for bugs and, given the lack of refrigeration and strange cuts of meat we ate, she had good reason.

But I never managed to love papaya, although with enough coaxing I would occasionally nibble on hers. For me, most breakfasts were cereal, toast and sweet, milky tea. My mother, on that one trip back to us, decided that I needed to be fortified and would make me a glass of eggnog every morning. While I loved the taste, I would become slightly nauseated soon after I drank it — we called that "bad feelings" and they were usually treated with the cooling, astringent scent of Limacol, made in B.G., a mixture of alcohol, aromatic oils and lime that was labelled "The Freshness of a Breeze in a Bottle." Nothing soothed bad feelings more than a little Limacol patted on the forehead or wafted gently near the nose.

Cookie would leave a light supper before she went home, but she never left before four o'clock tea, another ritual that linked us to the English rather than any Portuguese custom. We would look on delightedly as she cooled hot tea by pouring it in a wide arc from cup to cup, or we children would take it in small doses, poured into the saucer to cool, which we lifted carefully to our lips. She would serve a platter of small sandwiches or slices of pound cake and occasionally my favourite — a high, light angel food cake, presented on a glass plate.

Little wonder that, so many years later, the scent of simmering pepperpot or the spicy aroma of a glass of sorrel would trigger a flood of memories. It's a mysterious sensation, smell, the way it can transport us, suddenly and with such clarity, to a little window of time. Food was woven into the best of my childhood, the sense of well-being that enveloped me around that dining table.

We often ate cake at teatime, but the most memorable cakes appeared at Christmas. The preparations for Christmas baking began months before the holidays, when Granny made her rare appearance in the kitchen. An apron encircling her hefty middle, she would measure and mix the ingredients for her black cake, the Caribbean variation of the traditional English plum pudding. Dense and dark, filled with rum and fruit, black cake appeared only on special occasions like Christmas and weddings. The perfect base for an almond paste coating and hard icing, it took centre stage as a tiered wedding cake when my aunts married, and years later when I married. The alcohol ensured that it never spoiled, though I've always found its blackness too mysterious, its flavour too intense.

The cake I truly loved we called buldamel, known in Portuguese as *bolo de mel*, a honey cake with Madeiran roots, made in the Caribbean for generations, and another of Granny's Christmas treats. We ate many over the holiday season. A small yeast cake of molasses or honey, raisins, ground walnuts and almonds and warm Christmas spices like cloves and cinnamon, it was delicious with a cup of tea or a glass of port for the grownups. Like the black cake, a well-wrapped buldamel could last for months.

Though we were living in the tropics, Christmas in the house on Brickdam had an almost wintry flavour. My book-filled imagination conjured up the majesty of pine forests and snow because every year Grandfather imported a real evergreen tree, which sat in a corner of the window-lined front room. And every year we would hear the story of how, when the aunts and uncles were younger, the Christmas tree caught fire. It seems the teenage Auntie Lou, who had laboured for many hours decorating the tree, decided after the lights were on that she wanted snow on the branches. So she added mounds of cotton wool, which caught fire when they connected with the hot lights. The burning tree was promptly heaved out of a living-room window by an uncle. Relieved that they had averted a disaster — fire was the most destructive fact of life in this wood-filled town — they ran downstairs to douse the tree with buckets of water as it smouldered on the driveway below. "I didn't even make it to Midnight mass," Auntie Lou recalled. "Dad said, 'You can have your tree, but no more lights.'"

I never even noticed the lack of lights, nor did I care much about gifts under the tree, except for feeling jealous about all the toys George received the year he was sick. Our Christmas might have focused on churchgoing, but the highlight of the holiday took place at the dining table where we gathered for Christmas breakfast, a once-a-year feast simply known as garlic pork. Eaten all over the Caribbean, this traditional Christmas dish from Madeira and the Azores, *carne de vinha d'alhos* (meat in garlic marinade), can include bay leaves, cloves, thyme, paprika and hot pepper.

My family's Guyanese version — marinated, garlic-infused, cubed pork, simmered to soften, then seared until it gained a nut-brown finish on the outside — came under much scrutiny. The flavour of the pork steeped in vinegar, sprigs of fresh thyme, chopped garlic and red pepper was discussed from one year to the next — was it spicier, softer, too salty, more or less pungent than in years past? We all went off to mass on Christmas morning before eating, not only because we had to fast in order to receive Communion but also because once we had sat down to that meal, we could no longer be in the company of people who had not eaten the same breakfast. The odour of garlic seeped through our pores.

Every Christmas of my tropical childhood, the same ritual: before presents, before food, we would dress carefully for church on that special morning when the baby Jesus was born. Walking home, feeling light from lack of food and so good because we had done our Christmas duty, we could then play and open gifts while the adults prepared the feast — a celebratory dining table on which serving platters mounded with sizzling, aromatic garlic pork were laid out, along with slices of buttered bread. But while we children drank tea, the adults on this occasion sipped from small glasses of gin. The longing to head back home after that special Christmas mass, the anticipation of the festive table in the decorated house, eating the best breakfast ever, with our family and toys around us: pure joy.

When school was out in the hot summer months, Granny and Grandfather would send us out of the city, usually with a few cousins, to stay with Auntie Olga. She and her sister Lucille, called Lou by everyone, were now living with their young husbands along the Demerara River in one of the sugarcane plantations owned by British interests. Cane had been a huge source of income for the colonizers for more than three centuries; the British acquired the sugarcane fields when they took over the colony from the Dutch early in the nineteenth century.

Sunny days, balmy nights, but we never ventured into the fields under cultivation for sugarcane. Our playground was the part of the estate that housed the families of the dozen or so men employed as overseers — another colonial-laden name. In my childhood, more than a dozen similar plantations grew sugarcane with names that are redolent of Britain: Rose Hall and Wales or Reliance and Success, both named for merchant ships. Owned by British companies like Tate & Lyle and Booker Sugar Estates, they were all nationalized after independence in the mid-1970s to form the Guyana Sugar Corporation.

At Wales, the fresh air that streamed from the Demerara River cooled us, and there were no gates to enclose us near the house.

We would run and play on the nubbly lawns and roam around under the houses, each identically built on posts the height of one floor, allowing people to keep chickens or, in the case of my Uncle Arthur, who loved building things, to work on whatever he was constructing. Our Wales adventures so filled us up that, like most children, we could barely remember school days and our regular life at home in Georgetown.

Uncles Mike and Arthur were part of the team managing the growing and cutting of the sugarcane, which was then processed into sugar, named for the original colony of Demerara. First planted by the Dutch in the 1650s, sugarcane became the most lucrative crop in the colony, producing the famed golden brown Demerara sugar, with large crunchy grains and hints of toffee and molasses. Sugarcane was also the basis for Demerara rum. By the mid-1700s there were more than three hundred sugar factories, each one producing sugar as well as rich, dark rum from the molasses by-product.

But Wales was far enough away from Georgetown that sometimes just getting there was an adventure. One grey day, carrying a small bag filled with my pyjamas, shorts, and shirts, wearing sandals, I stood at the wharf in Georgetown with a few cousins and Auntie Olga. We clambered aboard an open boat in what felt like darkness for the hour-long trip about fifteen kilometres up the Demerara River to the western bank, moving at a tediously slow pace, rain lashing at our uncovered heads and arms.

This was a ferry in name only. Essentially, we were bobbing along in a large motorboat with a small wheelhouse, its deep deck crammed with passengers and their belongings, many cloth bags, boxes of food and an assortment of anxious children. It felt, in my imagination, like I was standing in a large container so deeply submerged that the river hovered precariously near the edge. I stood there, scared into silence, imagining that if just one more person came on board, all that water would slosh over the sides and start to fill the boat. But it never did, even with dark skies looming and the rain pelting.

The overseers' houses, each a square, one-storey building, were painted white with large roof overhangs to provide shade and windows on four sides open to the sea breeze. Built with outside stairs and small landings, the houses faced a packed dirt road that bordered a deep canal where huge metal barges, called punts, slowly floated from the cane fields carrying massive mounds of cut sugarcane. Unloaded at the factory at the top of the canal, the cane was then processed, leaving behind the delicious smell of burnt sugar which hung over the estate.

Each house was separated from the next by green lawns and mud-sided gutters, with the road and barge canal on one side and on the other a smaller waterway known as the "sideline," a conduit for overflow from the tidal river just beyond the high bank — the great, muddy Demerara. The small, deep gutters between the houses, also designed to carry runoff during the rainy season, were traversed by simple plank bridges. In the summer, however, the water was low in those gutters and so the high muddy sides became the perfect spot to dig for crabs. We would lie on our stomachs on the grass, sticks in hand, and peer over the edge, then poke the stick right beside one of the little holes that dotted the glistening interior walls of the gutter. In no time, little brown crabs would come spilling out. We didn't catch them or hurt them; the game was watching as the crabs scurried around, desperate to reach another hiding place.

On occasional summer nights, we would sleep over at Auntie Lou's. Her Scottish husband, Uncle Arthur, was tall and kind, though there was always a reserve about him, something hidden behind those eyes. Auntie Lou was more forthright. She had short brown hair, small eyes, and the classic imposing nose of most of my Portuguese relatives. But while she could be strict, I often detected an edge of humour in an exchange with her, a bit of a twinkle in her eye. She had a reputation as a fastidious housekeeper, so we never felt carefree when we stayed there. Everything had its place, and Auntie Lou made sure we realized that.

But we were prepared to forgo our usual liveliness if we could partake of the amazing food prepared by Auntie Lou's cook. An overseer's stipend included a cook or other household help, local women whose husbands likely worked in the sugarcane fields. Auntie Lou's cook won our hearts for her shrimp curry:

fat, juicy shrimp in a thick, peppery curry sauce served with freshly made roti.

One night when I was staying at Auntie Lou's, looking out the casement windows into the tropical darkness, the great river just beyond the ridge, listening to the calls of night birds and the chirp of insects, the radio played a song that squeezed my heart. "My prayer," sang my favourite group, the Platters, in smooth, melodious tones, "is to linger with you, at the end of the day, in a dream that's divine." These words were mysterious to me, but so full of meaning. Surrounded by family, was it loneliness that I felt? Did I miss my unknown parents? I remember feeling a strange melancholy as I looked through the uncurtained windows into the blackness, the Demerara River moving slowly through the night.

Like the windows in Georgetown, the windows at Wales had no screens, and insects occasionally flew in, especially at night when the lights were on. We were wary of mosquitos both because they disturbed our sleep and because they transmitted disease — my mother had contracted malaria as a child. So we all slept under mosquito nets, gauzy white netting set into a ring over the bed that made a filmy tent. I loved it, imagining I was in the Arabian Nights. Outdoors, we were occasionally bitten or stung, but no insect attack was as memorable as my two-year-old cousin Ian chomping one evening on a beetle that he had picked up off the floor near the standing lamp. You could hear the crunch.

Then one day, just after lunch, George and I were playing in the sandy space under Auntie Lou's house, near the spot where Uncle Arthur had secured his partially built boat with thick ropes to several of the columns under the building. As George dug industriously in the dirt, I began to notice a movement in one of the ropes above him that wound around the pillar, just a few feet from where he was playing. I was not yet wearing glasses and things were a bit fuzzy, but slowly it dawned on me — that undulating rope was a large snake.

Maybe this wasn't the boa constrictor I feared so much, but I knew danger when I saw it. I ran in a panic to call Uncle Arthur from his post-lunch siesta. George, somehow deaf to my yelling, remained completely focused on digging in the dirt while Uncle Arthur sprang into action, running downstairs with a large stick in one hand, cutlass — the Guyanese word for machete — in the other. Quickly, he hooked the snake with the stick, pulling it away from the column and flinging it into the grass. Using the scary, wide-bladed cutlass, Uncle Arthur proceeded to cut up the snake, although my eyes were squeezed so tightly shut, I saw almost nothing. My brother, unbothered, continued playing.

Running from house to house, going to the tennis courts, poking at the crabs, making mud pies, being teased by our uncles — these carefree times helped us avoid what was going on in the larger world, where the struggle for independence continued to grow. But even in our world of fun and games and occasional scrapes, we could be shocked out of our childish good cheer.

One morning, as we ate breakfast at Auntie Olga's sunny dining table, a strange yell came from the bedroom, then a thump. Even though it didn't sound like him, we knew it was Uncle Mike and we sat, paralyzed with fear, as Auntie Olga ran to him. What seemed like a long time later, we learned what she already knew: Uncle Mike was epileptic. He had suffered a seizure, one that would on very rare occasions short out the wiring in his brain. Without missing a beat, we adhered to the family practice around any traumatic event and never spoke of it again, even among ourselves.

British social life, writ small, existed here in the form of the Wales Club, a two-storey building at the top of the road lined by overseers' houses, set at the end of a long driveway. At the club, families could use the red clay tennis courts or sail from the dock that stretched out into the river. No sugarcane field worker ever set foot in here. We would sometimes be allowed to run up the road to greet Auntie Olga and Uncle Mike as they came back from drinks or hang out there while they played tennis.

Painted the usual tropical white with green trim, the club had wide verandahs on both floors that looked toward the tennis courts and the river. Inside, wood floors were polished to a high shine, the long bar sleekly varnished, the billiard tables covered in green baize. We wandered through the room as the men played billiards and couples sat at tables drinking Scotch, the ice clinking in their glasses. I recall mostly the outdoors, the texture of the clay courts, the high fences, breezes ruffling my frilly skirt.

But sunny Wales, like so much in my childhood paradise, had its own story of shame. These sugarcane estates were part of British Guiana's bitter history, a country where more than 85,000 slaves had been brought in chains over the years and forced to work for little food and a ramshackle place to live. Not allowed to practice their religion, they were whipped, raped, humiliated and sometimes killed. The cruelty flourished because absentee owners who took the profits left the managing of the estates to people described by Sir Benjamin d'Urban, Lieutenant Governor of Essequibo and Demerara in 1824, as "half educated men of little discretion or command over their own caprices; good planters perhaps — but quite unfit to have the charge of bodies of men."

Wales was one of those places, owned by John Gladstone, father of the future British prime minister William Gladstone. He acquired plantations in the early 1800s, often through mortgage defaults, and by the time Britain's Slavery Abolition Act of 1833 forced these slaveowners to free their chattels — which for a time many refused to do — he owned a number of large plantations. Like so many others, he was rewarded for his exploitative practice: the British government paid him about thirteen million pounds in current accounting for releasing the 2,508 slaves he owned.

But before the tide turned, a terrible price was paid to force that change in British Guiana. During the Demerara slave rebellion of 1823, which started as a non-violent protest for better conditions by up to 12,000 slaves, some of the slave owners had been taken prisoner for a few days. Even though they had not been hurt, the military responded with lethal brutality: they killed hundreds of slaves and later executed twenty-seven more. John Smith, the English vicar who aided the rebellion, was sentenced to death and died of consumption in prison, his sacrifice helping to promote the abolitionist cause.

Slavery ended a decade later and Wales was bought by the Booker Company, which already owned Booker's, the biggest of the trio of large department stores in Georgetown. By 1951, a few years after my birth, the Booker Company had begun its reconstruction led by Jock Campbell, a descendant of another family who had bought sugar estates at bargain prices. By all accounts an enlightened businessman who felt the need to practice social responsibility, Campbell recalled that on his first visit to British Guiana, he was "conscious that this had all been built on first of all slavery and then cheap labour." He was right: after the abolition of slavery, members of the Campbell family had successfully claimed what amounted to millions in today's currency for their several thousand slaves.

Under Campbell's leadership, the Booker Company negotiated the 1951 Commonwealth Sugar Agreement, a guarantee of fixed sugar imports and prices that included ways to improve the housing, health and social welfare of workers. Campbell's rehabilitation of the company informed a shrewd decision to become sponsor of the Booker Prize, the Commonwealth's most prestigious prize for English-language novels.

When we were children at play on the Wales estate, the dire exploitation of sugar workers didn't enter our minds. Did my aunts, uncles and cousins realize how close to the indentured labour side of the ledger we were on, despite our comfortable life? I knew nothing about the struggle Granny and Grandfather's families had undertaken, choosing to toil in El Dorado — as the country had been advertised to them in Madeira — rather than stay where they couldn't make a living. And while our people worked hard to acquire the trappings of privilege, we couldn't escape how most of the British ruling class viewed us — as uneducated and Catholic, therefore inferior.

Some scholars argue that the Portuguese did so well because we had actually been given preferential treatment by the British, who used us as a buffer against the emancipated Black population. And here's the irony: our own country, Portugal, had long ago initiated the Atlantic slave trade. But whatever catastrophe brought us here, however we were used or misused, there's no doubt we considered British Guiana our home. In my childish view, our life here was a beautiful mixture of Portuguese family ties combined with British cultural practices and the Caribbean's colour and warmth. We were in the garden, after all.

chapter 3

the marriage of frank and lily

My family emigrated to British Guiana because of the demise of the slave trade. When slavery ended, and those who survived among the tens of thousands of Africans brought to the country were grudgingly released, they scrambled to free themselves from work in the cane fields. So the British needed labour in those festering sugar plantations, and looked around for poor families who were desperate to leave difficult circumstances for opportunity, however uncertain.

The first ships brought workers from Madeira, a mountainous island off the coast of Morocco formed at the top of a dormant volcano rising about six kilometres from the ocean floor. Portuguese voyagers had landed there in the early 1400s and, after only seventy-five years of settlement, the island had become the world's foremost producer of sugar. It also became an important centre of shipping and navigation because of its location in the Atlantic shipping lanes. The ancestors of my great-grandparents would have been tending sugarcane or serving customers in one of the shops that dotted the growing town of Funchal.

The Portuguese had already travelled huge distances in terrible conditions to escape poverty. In the fifteenth century, peasants and fishermen formed the majority of settlers on the island, a gift from the king to his son, the legendary maritime explorer Prince Henry the Navigator. Some settlers fled Portugal to escape the ravages of the Black Death. Others made the journey to Madeira after the cataclysmic Lisbon earthquake of 1755.

Hardworking and entrepreneurial these ordinary folk might have been, but those who ran Portugal's empire wielded power with a cruel hand. The world's leading purveyors of slaves, whose bodies they sold to the Americas and whose labour they exploited in the Madeiran cane fields, the Portuguese profited from their colonies, where slaves did the backbreaking work of excavating, harvesting and transporting the cane. By the sixteenth century, African slaves made up ten per cent of the total population of Madeira. And even though slavery was abolished on the island in 1775, the Portuguese continued the practice for nearly another century, mainly in Brazil.

Madeira was a leader in cane production, but the fertile cane fields were eked out at a massive cost. The island was so wet that the early settlers built levadas, 3,100 kilometres of narrow canals, to irrigate the drier and flatter terrain on the lower parts of the island. It was also so heavily forested — the word madeira means "wood" in Portuguese — that many acres were burned and plant species destroyed to create an environment for growing sugarcane. One forested area burned slowly, wetly, for seven years. Luckily, some of the mountainous regions were so inaccessible that the island still contains one of the last and largest old-growth forests in Europe.

Perhaps because the ruling classes were so focused on exploitation, deforestation and soil depletion soon led to the end of Portugal's dominance in sugar production. In less than a century, the cane fields were ruined and no longer producing. Then the Madeirans began planting grapes on the island to produce the famed fortified wine which soon became popular all over the world. Madeira was the favourite wine of colonial Americans in the eighteenth century, and by the late nineteenth century St. Petersburg vied with London for the highest consumption of the dark red wine.

But diseases crippled the vines and in the mid-1800s a blight of powdery mildew decimated them. Production ceased and those Portuguese peasants were desperate to find work in order to feed their families. They had the skills to grow both grapes and sugar cane, developed over three centuries on the land.

It must have been relatively easy, then, for the British plantation owners in this colony, looking for workers to replace the emancipated slaves, to lure those Madeiran peasants across the North Atlantic. At this point there was a long-standing alliance between the British and the Portuguese, and so it began: in May

1835, after a voyage of seventy-eight days, the Louisa Baillie docked in Demerara with forty Madeiran emigrants bound for sugar plantations. By 1882, more than 30,000 Portuguese had fled Madeira, significantly reducing its population. The majority made their way to British Guiana, among them two Portuguese families, their surnames Faria and Gomes, stereotypical in their adherence to family, religion and hard work.

Their offspring would become my grandparents. He was Francisco Gomes, known as Frank; she was Leolinda Faria, called Lily. Few pictures survive of the couple in their younger years, but there is one sepia-toned photo in my possession showing a group of young men and women formally posed, the women in long skirts, the moustachioed men in shirts with high collars and flat-topped straw hats. My grandmother stands among them in half profile, her hair coiled in an ornate bun. She wears a prim blouse, her firm jaw shadowing a high collar. Her skirt, cinched at the waist, is full length, her ankle boots tightly laced. Though the rest, sitting and standing, are expressionless, she is looking at the camera with a slight smile.

The bounty paid to the planters by the British government for each immigrant brought to the sugarcane plantations guaranteed a two- to four-year period of indentured labour. Soon thousands of Madeirans arrived with their families, so desperate to leave that entire communities were abandoned. They faced terrible conditions here as well; diseases like dysentery and yellow fever killed many of the early immigrants. The death rate was so high — up to fifty per cent in the first two decades — that at one point the Portuguese government halted emigration. Nevertheless the immigrants persisted, and throughout the 1800s they chartered ships from Madeira bringing cargos of salt cod and wine, as well as new families.

They were enterprising, these Portuguese, and soon had a reputation as wily and hard-working. Even though they made up less than five per cent of the population of British Guiana around the time my grandfather was born in 1895, they had achieved a status beyond their numbers. Because once the indenture was worked off, most of them fled the brutal conditions on the sugarcane plantations for Georgetown and focused their entrepreneurial skills on retail businesses. They were so successful that Guyanese history records at least one mini-uprising by the descendants of African slaves against the Portuguese control of local commerce.

The Madeiran emigrants brought flair and expertise to the country. By the mid-1800s they owned most of the rum shops, a dominance they maintained well into the twentieth century. A few decades later, Portuguese entrepreneurs were property owners, merchants of every sort from rum to leather to timber, ironmongers and ship chandlers, boot and shoemakers, coach builders and more. "The rise of the Portuguese in this colony from a state of most abject poverty to one of comparative affluence, and to the possession, in many instances, of thousands of dollars within the space of a few years, is one of the most remarkable occurrences in modern colonial history," writes Sister Mary Noel Menezes, a scholar of Portuguese migration.

She paints an indelible portrait of the people who crossed the ocean to forge a life in this new world: "The Madeiran emigrant, then, did not arrive in British Guiana devoid of everything but his conical blue cloth cap, coarse jacket, short trousers and his rajao (banjo) … He brought with him a background history in agriculture, a flair for business, as well as the culture and mores of his island home, a replica of the mother country, Portugal."

In British Guiana, the Madeirans practiced their religion with zeal, building their first church in 1861. They created societies for the poor and sick, competed enthusiastically in sports like boxing, cricket and cycling, and expressed their love of music by creating bands and orchestras. The Portuguese Club, where my mother and her siblings were members, was founded in 1925, and it's likely my grandfather got his well-developed calf muscles from membership in the Vasco da Gama Cycling Club, established when he was just a toddler.

But while they held on to their language throughout the nineteenth century, by the twentieth century it had been subsumed by English, the language of the colony. The Portuguese were always outsiders, not always considered European or even white by their colonial overlords; records show that in the 1891 census, "Portuguese from Madeira" was listed as a separate category.

The clannishness and ambition that helped them succeed as shopkeepers and landowners bred resentment from the Black population. I wonder how many Madeirans realized they were being used by the British as a buffer, to withhold ownership from the Blacks.

I would be sitting in a chair nearby, legs swinging, sometimes with an open book, listening to my aunts chatter. I loved their childhood memories best, when someone would remember "Grandmother," one of those hard-working Portuguese women who believed in their role as wives and mothers. As it turns out, while my great-grandmothers achieved both those goals, they spent most of their lives as widowed entrepreneurs.

Grandfather's parents were among the emigrants who soon became small business owners. They opened a successful rum shop which his mother, Mary, took over after his father's early death. Later she took her son's advice and bought houses in the town, occasionally pointed out to me during one of our Sunday drives.

Granny's mother, Claudina Fernandes, also owned shops and property in her later years. Born of Madeiran parents in 1872 in a farming area near the Demerara River called West Bank, she appears in one formal family photograph as a young mother, a pretty, buxom woman in a full-length light cotton dress with a tiered skirt, tightly belted. She is standing solemnly with husband, son, daughter and new bald baby, who is just sitting up in a wicker chair. Behind him stands my grandmother, who might be four or five years old, leaning on the back of the chair in a pale dress with lace at the sleeves and hem, her light brown ringlets held at both sides of her face with white flowers, her little fingers just touching her mother's hand. Her brother Jose, in a stiff collar and buttoned jacket, stands beside the chair, his father's hand casually upon his shoulder.

The most arresting figure is the father, my great-grandfather José Gomes de Faria, born in 1871 in Santa Luzia, Madeira. His jacket is open, a thin dark tie encircles his stand-up collar and his other arm is bent, draped casually on the backdrop behind his wife, fingers dangling. Unlike everyone else in the photograph, his body is relaxed, untroubled; there's even a hint of a smile underneath the waxed moustache on his narrow face. He is a rum shop owner and a successful one at that, with two shops and a line of his own spirits. He had encountered Claudina when he visited her home with one of her brothers; their meetings were likely strictly chaperoned, as was the custom of the time. He seemed to have a touch of whimsy, naming one of his shops the Green and Gold Rum Shop, and died young of a heart attack. "My mother told me that he drank too much of his own liquor," Auntie Olga said.

By the age of forty-eight, Claudina was a widow, and because it was inappropriate for a woman to run this type of business, the eldest boy took over the rum shops. But he wasn't a good businessman. "When Grandmother realized he was spending too much of money," Olga said, using a Guyanese turn of phrase, "one of the other brothers suggested she sell everything, give each one of them their share, and buy property that she could handle, like houses. And that's what she did."

The aunts often hinted that Granny wasn't very fond of her mother and doted on her father. But when she was overwhelmed by her growing brood, Granny sent both Auntie Thelma and my mother to stay with their grandmother for many months at a time, an experience they recalled with pleasure. She was hard-working and kind and she made the most delicious coffee, my mother said, grinding her own beans and, before the coffee brewed, adding "a tip of butter." I imagine the deep yellow South American butter, melting and swirling in the steaming cup.

They didn't have such warm feelings about Grandfather's mother. "Look," Auntie Olga said, "she sent her own daughter back to Portugal to live with relatives, and she never saw her again!" I never found out more about great-aunt Mathilda.

The first in their family to abandon Madeira, the brothers José, Antonio and Emanuel Gomes de Faria had fled conscription in the Portuguese army where many young men were taken, sometimes by force. They left their homes in Funchal, likely in the late 1880s. According to Granny, the boys' father bribed the ship's captain to smuggle one of them aboard in a barrel of onions.

I came along two generations later and, growing up, heard little about Madeira except for a certain pride about lace and wine, and one story about a family heirloom, a gold starburst brooch dotted with diamonds and pearls that was connected to Portuguese royalty, found in a park in Madeira by one of Granny's uncles. It had fallen under some bushes, the story goes, where it lay until he found it. I imagined some peasant fellow trudging through the park one day, who might have been fearful that, if he returned the brooch, he would be in trouble. The story thrilled me. Could we have actually ended up with a jewel belonging to a queen or princess, I wondered.

My grandparents never discussed our place in the society of British Guiana, but I never heard the country described as a way station to somewhere else. We identified ourselves as Guyanese even though, as in so many colonial settings, we lived in a fractured cultural environment. By the time I appeared, the country was a mix of Indian, Black, Indigenous, Chinese and European, a cook-up of cultures. But despite the success of those Madeiran immigrants as merchants and landowners, they received little social acknowledgment from the well-heeled British in the country, who ran the show politically and made lots of money from the production of sugar and extraction of bauxite. Most important, the ruling classes tended to keep to themselves socially, which might have upset the Portuguese but didn't curtail their drive.

Along with adopting, embracing even, the customs of the colonizers, we carried on with our attachment to extended family, foods and of course religion, true for every immigrant group arriving in a strange land. But while speaking English made sense — of course we learned the language of the colonizers — within one generation we had lost our Portuguese language. Even my grandparents only knew a few words. I can only think that these pragmatic immigrants didn't feel their numbers were strong enough and that it was in their best interest to remove any obstacles from their participation in the British-run society. So the language had to go.

And even though by the beginning of the twentieth century the Portuguese were well established in British Guiana and many, like my two aunts, married men from the U.K., they continued to stand apart. So it was no wonder they felt adrift by the time of the struggle for independence in the 1950s and 1960s. The colony that we had called home for a century was about to undergo a radical transformation where the majority would rule, and rightly so. As the Afro-Guyanese and Indo-Guyanese prepared to take over the country, the Portuguese were left with an uncertain future, and Granny and Grandfather, like many others, would end up leaving home. Some went to the U.S. but mainly they settled in Canada or Britain.

In the early days of independence, incompetent leadership made a mess of the country and especially Georgetown. In my childhood, the city was true to V.S. Naipaul's sense of a dream of tropical architecture, its wooden buildings decorated with gingerbread, fretwork and rows of tall louvred windows. But the struggles that erupted in the 1960s left both buildings and gardens in a state of disrepair and only fifty years later did the country begin to recover. The present is much rosier, though no less fraught: an early foray into ecotourism has now been overshadowed by the discovery of offshore oil.

My grandfather was the eldest of five children, four boys and a girl. The match between my serious grandfather and my grandmother Lily, sweet-faced and gentle, lasted a lifetime. They spent nearly seventy years in Georgetown, where they raised their ten children, then my brother and myself, and another two decades in Canada, where they lived in Ontario with one or another of their children. They died there, a few years apart, both aged ninety-two.

Granny seemed old to me when I was a child, but she was only in her late fifties. I didn't know much about the young woman who bore those children in the first dozen years of her marriage. The Granny I knew was always carefully dressed, hair curled and brushed, and her house was so well organized that I couldn't imagine what it would have been like with ten young children running about.

She was Mrs. Frank Gomes, always standing proudly by his side. They were a couple in an utterly traditional sense: he was the breadwinner while she ruled the home, the children and household staff. They shared an abiding hope in their Catholic faith, offering to God whatever sorrows or hardships came their way.

Granny didn't have much to say about the world but knew everything there was to know about the family. We called her

Granny while her children gave her the more formal title of "Mother." She had a classic, handsome face: long straight nose, thin lips, kind eyes behind her glasses. She was the best example I ever knew of an iron fist inside a velvet glove, soft-spoken but determined to get her way. Granny liked being the wife of someone important and was devoted to her family, but I wondered later what lessons she took from her religion when she encountered the poverty and injustice layered into colonial life.

Maybe because she had come from peasant stock, Granny could be imperious with those she considered of lesser status. In other words, bossy with the servants. But she could be kind, too, and dependable; Cookie stayed with her for years. She always deferred to Grandfather, although they would sometimes exchange impatient words. To me she felt welcoming, comfortable, with her ample bosom and sensible shoes. She knew her duty and to whom she owed everything — to Jesus, to the Lord.

My mother, Gwendoline Dorothy Gomes, was the oldest girl of these ten siblings. In later years, when I would sit listening to my aunts and uncles reminisce or as I pored over the trove of photographs in albums or stuffed into envelopes, my impression was of an idyllic youth. I visualized the boys as adventurous and strong, the girls as energetic and good-looking, in white shorts with strong white teeth. Although, in truth, it was only my mother as a young woman whose life I imagined.

Ten lively young people meant a lot of high spirits and sometimes difficult times, like Uncle Charlie's motorcycle accident when he was laid up with a broken collarbone, my mother's childhood bouts with malaria or Uncle Stanley's childhood stroke that left him in a coma. Granny nursed him and, the story goes, never gave up hope in the power of prayer. She was right; in a few weeks he struggled out of his coma and eventually recovered.

The siblings spent their time at the rowing club or the tennis club, with lots of swimming or games or cheering on the cricket players — my father was one. The photos document their adventures at the pool or on the courts and occasionally capture the young women in lovely, drapey dresses and strings of pearls, the young men in cuffed pants, crisp shirts and ties. The Gomes children lived in a large, fine home with Mother and Daddy. They looked like they hadn't a care in the world.

But they occupied a middle ground in this tropical life in which they were neither colonizers nor labourers. A second-generation Guyanese, Grandfather had assimilated well, at least on the surface. We followed many Portuguese cultural traditions, but there was a certain Stockholm syndrome, an attachment to the practices of the ruling class. We stopped for tea and cake at four o'clock, played cricket and ignored the huge class divisions based on race. It was unsettling for me to hear Auntie Olga speak with pride of never wanting to marry a Portuguese man, implying somehow that they were not worthy. Much better to choose British or Canadian, the aunts said.

I never questioned the bizarre contradiction in my family: what looked like acceptance of an individual, whatever their colour, coupled with a disdain for those less fortunate, especially the Black population who often did the manual labour around the place. Then at university in Canada, I began to read about colonialism, and I began to talk back. After the shocking revelations of Franz Fanon's *The Wretched of the Earth*, I had slowly begun to understand that we were complicit in looking and acting like the colonizers.

Someone would occasionally raise the spectre of the lazy Black who would rather drink rum under the shade of the banana tree than do a day's work. "Why should they care about work?" I argued hotly with Uncle Mike. Why should the descendants of slaves care, I declared, when under colonialism they would never have the opportunity to live better lives? I never did speak that way with Grandfather, even as I became an adult and he an old man living in Canada, perhaps because I never heard him criticize any Black person he knew. In any case, how could I face being disappointed by his response?

Every night, my grandparents' fingers travelled across rosary beads — hers white, his black — as they sat on their rocking chairs in the tower, its small altar to the baby Jesus tucked away in one corner. There were crucifixes or holy pictures above the doorways to most of the bedrooms, and Granny would always end letters in her beautiful, rounded script with the wish, "May God bless you and keep you and the Blessed Virgin smile upon you." Every Sunday, we would follow our grandparents on the walk to Brickdam Cathedral just down the street from the house, and every Lent we gave up sweets.

They didn't wear their religious observations loudly — they entertained, enjoyed good food, Grandfather loved his Scotch and, until his sixties, his cigarettes. And while they expected us to comply, to go to mass and to participate in the Catholic rituals of first communion and confirmation, they prayed and said the rosary alone, at night. We didn't say grace at every meal nor were the children expected to kneel and pray regularly, although Granny taught us a bedtime prayer that always terrified me: "There are four corners round my bed / There are four angels round my head / One to sing, one to pray / And two to take my soul away." Take my soul away? Does that mean I could die during the night? The point of that was never explained.

Nevertheless, for me anyway, the rituals had an impact. Who could not be moved when contemplating the Stations of the Cross, the horrible miseries on the path toward death trod by poor, struggling Jesus? And the Hail Marys and Our Fathers we were told to say after blurting out our whispered sins during confession really did feel like forgiveness.

The practice of churchgoing was central; it anchored our week and made Sunday into a special day, partly because we dressed up for the occasion. The girls wore puffy-sleeved cotton dresses and hats tied under the chin with elastic or ribbons. I always carried my favourite purse — a small white plastic rectangle whose handle I enjoyed slowly peeling apart. I thought my brother George adorable in a shirt and patterned tie, his white suit made of a shiny material we called sharkskin. Grandfather favoured a light grey suit, and Granny would be turned out in a flowered print dress, sometimes with a bolero top, a matching belt around her ample belly. Her hat sometimes had a high crown but most of her hats were fitted, with matching veils. And she always, always wore gloves.

Granny had gloves for every outfit and Sunday was the day she wore them, a practice she carried into old age, although she put away her sheer tropical gloves when she came to Canada. These transported me every time I saw them, a delicious spectacle of colour and texture. When Granny died, Auntie Olga asked me if I wanted the gloves, not realizing the power they had to conjure up those calm, sunny Sundays. I own them now: the black lace gloves she paired with a black lace dress, the butter-yellow gloves in cotton eyelet, bright yellow organza gloves with frill, crocheted gloves in lemon yellow, the pink lace gloves embroidered around the wrist, the navy organza gloves with a row of tiny flat pearl buttons that she wore with a blue and white dress and matching jacket.

Dressed in her Sunday best, Granny would walk into church, back straight, looking into the middle distance, a self-conscious frisson in her movement betraying her awareness that she was someone important in these surroundings. Grandfather, also serious, was more relaxed. With Granny leading the way, we would make our way slowly to the front of the church, Grandfather shepherding me and my brother, maybe several cousins. Eventually I learned to love the Latin mass, could recite many parts of it even as a child, and once I had taken my first communion would reverently stick out my tongue to receive the host, careful not to touch it with my teeth.

First communion was a big deal, treated as rite of passage in our little Catholic world, but for me the ritual was secondary to the lace dress with a tiered skirt, pearl-studded crown and veil. Since these were not store-bought items, the type of lace trim, the length of the cascade, the shape of the neck and the pattern of the veil each had to be decided in consultation with the dressmaker. I really didn't have much to say, I liked it all, and in any case, there was no arguing about the finished results if the grownups approved. The ensemble, including little white gloves, new white shoes and socks were marred only by a playtime fall just days before the ceremony. The sticking plaster on my knee made it hard to kneel and blighted my formal Communion photo.

Those were the days of fish on Fridays and fasting before mass. Even in young adulthood, when I had rejected Catholicism and its anti-women strictures, I continued to love the contemplative atmosphere of a church and the cadence of the Latin mass. I carried my religious fervour from childhood into early adolescence, entranced by the story of the Portuguese children who had seen the Virgin Mary at Fatima. Hoping for a vision of my own in a corner of my Canadian bedroom, I was at the same time terrified that seeing a miracle would mean I had to become a nun, a prospect that filled me with dread. And I continued during those early years in Canada to pray for my own mother, who never went to church even though my brother and I were always delivered there on Sunday mornings. She will go to hell, I thought, worried even after she told me with calm certainty that it's not whether you go to church that matters, it's how you live your life.

Granny had raised ten girls and boys, but when she cared for us, my brother and I were the only children living at home. My aunts and uncles were adults, a few had gone to Canada, another to live in Barbados and the youngest son had been sent to school in England. Uncle Clement was living next door and the youngest daughters, Olga and Lou, were still at home but nearing marriage. I remember Uncle Charlie early on, riding his motorcycle with his buddies, but by the time I was eight, he had joined his siblings in Canada.

I never thought of Granny as vain or particularly acquisitive; she was reserved rather than friendly, self-conscious I think, and I was never sure why. Once the children were born and raised, did she feel less relevant? Was she uneasy in the more monied segment of society, she the daughter of shopkeepers? She didn't have much to say beyond the running of her household, and even that looked less like a job with servants in the picture.

She was overweight until her eighties, when she slimmed down so much that she could look quite svelte in a pantsuit. But my memories of her in Georgetown include a rather nasty girdle, with a row of fasteners from pubis to underneath her breasts, that she would lay out on her bed and then, lying on her back on top of it, reach around and tighten the straps around her body. A metaphor of subjugation.

Is this what Granny wanted from her life? In my self-absorbed young adulthood, questioning the role of women, I asked myself whether it was enough, making family the centre of your existence. But in those childhood years, where would I have been without her care? There was a quietness about her, no excessive shows of feeling except in her letters, where she would express her love, ask me to do well and pray, and always ask God to help me and keep me.

She also tended to make more of her hardships than her daughters considered acceptable. Her fixation on her aching knees or a pain somewhere in her body stood in clear contrast to Grandfather's quiet stoicism. Her daughters thought her spoiled by her good fortune, and I remember wondering why she would complain about the servants or the quality of a meal, those very luxuries that made her life easy.

But, outwardly at least, once my grandparents had arrived in Canada, she seemed to accept the change without making a fuss. There was no question, living in Canada didn't resemble Georgetown at all — they had left the big house behind, along with nearly everything in it. Auntie Olga observed that even though they had brought several trunks full of belongings, most of the beautiful silver and family heirlooms never made it to Canada. "She brought all her shoes," Olga said, shaking her head. Even that fabulous mahogany table was sold off, despite Uncle Frank's efforts to have it shipped to Canada.

Granny and Grandfather lived their final years together in a little flat above Auntie Lou's garage. Their children were always around; family ties continued to bind them. And wherever she was, her deep love of God never left her, nor her rituals. She said the rosary every night throughout her life, although faith didn't seem to be enough when Grandfather died. We had gathered at his wake in one of the chapels of a nondescript Ontario funeral home and someone gently led Granny to the open coffin. Seeing him there, she became so distraught that for a moment I thought she was going to climb in. "Frank? Frank?" she cried, reaching for him.

After he was gone and she went to live at Auntie Olga's, a contemporary flat-roofed home surrounded by so much glass and greenery that it felt underwater, I stayed overnight a few times and was distressed to hear Granny in the next room, crying out in the night. She said she tossed and turned a lot, and one morning described a dream of seeing her son, my Uncle Charlie, who had recently died from a brain tumour, standing in a doorway.

She knew her own death was approaching, and I realized that either she was deeply fearful of death, or expressing openly what many people hide from others. It was a childish fear, almost, because what is stronger than belief in an afterlife where you meet your benevolent Maker? But she was afraid, and it scared me.

I loved her without question, even when as a teenager I began to criticize her passivity and her abject devotion to this unseen master. But she had given us so much. Never, during our years in Georgetown, had my brother and I ever felt unwanted or a burden to our grandparents — except for the incident where I spilled the milk. And even in their traditional world where the roles of women and men seemed so determined, I remember how happy she was, how she held me and hugged me, when I came first in class at the Ursuline convent.

I was never privy to the romance that bound her to Grandfather. When I was older, I learned that the young man, in his early twenties, would bicycle out to Pleasance, the village outside Georgetown where Granny's family lived, to visit her. Throughout their married life, they slept side by side in separate beds and displays of affection between them were particularly sweet for their rarity. But the two of them were a constant: a portly couple who bickered but rarely fought, and who treated each other with a quiet benevolence.

One Sunday, after sixty years of marriage, in the Ontario town where they lived, he put on a new grey suit and she wore a patterned dress and jacket which fitted nicely on her smaller body, complete with hat and, of course, gloves. With dozens of family members in attendance, they walked down the aisle of the local Catholic church and, in front of the priest, renewed their marriage vows.

Grandfather was a methodical man whose daily routines underpinned my life. Most mornings, he would rouse us from sleep by pulling the little toes that poked from the bottom of our bunk beds. "Rise and shine!" he would call out as we yelped, our toes smarting. Other times, he would rub his scratchy beard on our cheeks as we giggled and squealed.

He exuded a sense of quietude and care, whether it was taking a walk or a drive, at the dinner table or with friends on a Saturday afternoon. He wore lightweight suits during the week, on weekends favouring khaki pants and short-sleeved cotton shirts, often plaid, his nut-brown arms covered in a light fuzz of hair, a wristwatch always a bit loose on his left wrist. Small and wiry like many Portuguese, even though he grew heavier in late middle age, he often looked serious. I thought him very strong.

Grandfather had a special pre-bedtime ritual which I regularly witnessed because the bathroom sink was located in the corner of the central upstairs landing near the boys' room, where I often slept. In his undershirt and striped cotton pyjamas, tightened with a drawstring, Grandfather would lean over the sink to wash his face and then vigorously brush the hair that encircled his very bald pate. Going to the tall cupboard on the landing, he would uncork a long-necked dark bottle and take a swig of a mystery liquid that I believed was honey, though Auntie Olga assured me later that it was rum. Then he would brush his teeth, gargle noisily and be ready to join Granny in the tower for their nightly sojourn in their rocking chairs.

Grandfather was never a disciplinarian to George and me, although he wasn't a pushover either. But with his own children, he was always strict. His daughters adored him, but I grew to realize that his sons were somewhat cowed by him. And while I understood growing up that our comfortable life was the result of Grandfather's hard work, I can't recall anyone discussing the value of education. In our family, the women did secretarial work when they weren't stay-at-home mothers, and most of my uncles had trades or ran small businesses; none became professionals.

My most successful uncle, Steve, went to sea at the age of sixteen and worked his way up in the Canadian Coast Guard to become captain of the country's most sophisticated icebreakers. His brother Clement, the oldest, was the only one who stayed in British Guiana, perhaps because he had ties to the country that went beyond the familial — he had become leader of the Sea Scout movement there and was feted for these accomplishments. But he too left in the late 1960s.

Thelma, Stanley, my mother and Charlie had all followed Steve to Canada, joined by Olga and Lou just a few years before my brother and I arrived in 1959. No question, they were wise to leave the country ahead of the political upheavals and economic uncertainty that forced ninety per cent of educated Guyanese to leave between 1965 and 2000. Guyana, with up to half of its population now living abroad, has one of the highest levels of "brain drain" of any country in the world.

Some Saturday mornings, we're given permission to visit Grandfather at the department store that he manages. There are three big department stores in the city — the others are Fogarty's and Bookers, which is British-owned and by far the biggest. But I remember only my grandfather's, a Portuguese-owned store named G. Bettencourt & Co.

The building on Water Street is three stories high and half a block long, the sidewalk level shaded by the extended upper floors, supported with square columns. My cousins and I visit on our way to Brown Betty's, a busy soda fountain that is a block away from the store. We are planning to treat ourselves when we're there and need to stop by for a bit of spending money. Cash in hand, walking through the main floor, we open a nondescript wooden door and head along a corridor, then out through the loading bays where the white delivery trucks are parked, the ones driven by Sonny, Manu and Innis. "Hello, Miss Donna," someone calls out. We wave as we pass by, making our way outside and across the road.

Then we enter the chocolate-brown doorway of Brown Betty's — a dark room, buzzing with people, chrome-ringed stools lined up under a long counter. The smell is unforgettable, a chocolatey aroma that saturates the place and flavours the chilled sweetness of the thick, pale malted milk served there, unrivalled for the rest of my life. After we're satiated with malted milk and atmosphere, we return the same way and enter Grandfather's store. The interior of the building is full of glass-topped counters and racks of clothing hanging along the walls. But we're not interested in store-bought clothes: a dressmaker comes to our house twice a year and makes all our clothes except for the underwear that Granny buys for us. In any case, my focus is mainly on the cotton candy machine, a novelty on the first floor that doles out delicious pink spun sugar.

I'm happiest on the top floor where few people go, with its raw wood flooring, full of dry goods and hardware. This is my grandfather's kingdom, his office a large, raised platform with low walls in the middle of the cavernous open space. I climb three or four stairs into his office, and there sits Grandfather at a huge desk, piled with columns of papers. He can work while surveying the scene all around him, like being inside a fenced garden with papers and files instead of flowers, a landscape of counters encircling the huge room. Here, goods are stacked on floor-to-ceiling shelves and dust motes float lazily in the light streaming through high windows. I am captivated by the size of the place, the woodsy smell, the security I feel being with Grandfather.

He carried himself with dignity in all the time I knew him, a shrewd, careful man who never showed any sense of worry or anxiety. I never knew how much he had to ingratiate himself to the British who ran the country. But here was a clue: a photograph taken while he was on a buying trip to England, having travelled by ship across the Atlantic. Grandfather, in a long dark coat and slouch hat, looked so sombre, so serious, a stranger to the cold English landscape.

In my eyes, Grandfather was confident and knowing. My grandparents weren't the hugging sort, but they enveloped us with care. And from Grandfather there was one thing I knew for sure: we could count on him because George and I were family. So it came as a surprise when I learned that both Granny and Grandfather seemed to have grown distant from members of their own families. Grandfather had a few brothers who rarely visited and a sister who had been sent back to Madeira and was never seen again. He supported another brother who my aunts never knew existed until they were teenagers. Was it because Grandfather had made the climb to the upper middle classes and felt this relationship would tarnish his image? It makes me sad to think so.

Grandfather was well established in his community when I was a child. I recall one Sunday afternoon when he left me and a couple of cousins sitting in the car outside an ornate three-storey wooden building, one of his clubs. He had detoured from our Sunday drive to drop in, maybe to have a drink with friends. He never explained why he needed to be there.

Thinking about it in later years, I wondered what they were discussing, those men — they were always men only. Were they worrying then about what would happen when the British left, which was in the works? Did they envision the coming decline?

Unlike Granny, whose every action and concern focused on family and religion, Grandfather's relationships extended to friends. Every Saturday afternoon, returning from our weekly fill of the Saturday matinee, we could climb the inner front stairs to the first floor and find Grandfather in one of the armchairs along the gallery, deep in conversation with Mr. Morris Fernandes, a white Portuguese businessman, and Sir Donald Jackson, a Black legal scholar. They exuded comfort in each other's company, glasses of Scotch and soda and cigarettes in hand. Although I made a point of playing around nearby, soaking up the atmosphere, I don't recall what they spoke about. But I knew what they were saying was important.

I admired Sir Donald's quietness and his good nature. He would sit in a straight-backed chair beside his friends, leaning forward slightly, in a dark suit. He always seemed to be listening intently, speaking softly. Later I would learn that he had been Chief Justice of the Windward and Leeward Islands and then Speaker of the pre-independent Legislative Assembly of British Guiana. No matter — for us kids, the most important detail was that he had been knighted by the Queen. Nothing was more prestigious than that.

By his side, sinking into the largest chair, sat Mr. Fernandes, a fat man with thinning hair who wore a white suit and would often pause to mop his brow. He had a round face to go with his body and we knew his family well — his daughter, Margaret, was a good friend of my Auntie Olga's, and taught in a little kindergarten farther down our street. I had attended for a time, joining the girls wearing navy blue pinafores, the boys in blue shorts and short-sleeved white shirts. Auntie Olga assisted Margaret there sometimes, though it turned out she wasn't calm enough to handle a group of small children, especially her own niece. I can't think what I would have done, but on one occasion she chased me around the room. I think her teaching career was put on hold after that.

But the focus of those afternoons wasn't family or business. No, these guys got together to talk politics, which they did affably — even though as time went on, and the country wrestled with independence, both Grandfather and Mr. Fernandes would leave the country, as did most of the Portuguese and Chinese who had lived there for generations. Sir Donald, on the other hand, would be a player in the formation of a new government for the newly independent Guyana.

Forced to make those monumental decisions about leaving or staying, the old friends went their separate ways. I often wondered whether they kept in touch, since letter writing would have been a practice they understood. If those letters existed, I have never found them, and never thought to ask Grandfather. Could the three friends have foreseen the political turmoil that would ensue? Could they have imagined that the British, in a bid to avert rule by the democratically elected, Communist-inspired

People's Progressive Party and its leader, Cheddi Jagan, would first suspend the country's new constitution and then embark on a classic campaign to destroy the PPP — pitting ethnic groups against each other?

Then, when the British finally gave the PPP the right to rule, the Americans wouldn't have it. British Guiana became a Cold War battleground, racked with ethnic and racial divisions. American intervention paved the way to power for the leader of the opposition, Forbes Burnham, whose eventual authoritarian rule brought decades of misery and poverty.

No wonder people left. By the mid-1960s, after several scary years of racial turmoil when buildings were burned and Grandfather slept with a gun under his pillow, my grandparents came to Canada for the remainder of their lives.

Grandfather died in 1988 and Granny a few years later. I never knew whether Mr. Fernandes had followed his daughter Margaret to Canada, but Sir Donald Jackson continued his important work, and eventually was named a justice in the Federal Supreme Court of the West Indies. When he died in November 1981, he was eulogized with a number of lengthy speeches in the National Assembly of the country that was no longer my home.

Like so many Portuguese, Grandfather liked hard work, both physical and mental, but what set him apart, I thought, was his spiritual turn of mind. He prayed every day, occasionally quoted the Bible, and subscribed to the notion that being wealthy and powerful were not what mattered in life. His favourite saying, although he never told us it was from the apostle Mark, would be shared whenever the need arose. "What does it profit a man if he gains the whole world," Grandfather would intone, "yet suffers the loss of his own soul?"

Sometimes, as he stood before the bathroom mirror on the hall landing, we would hear him speak out. "What to do?" Grandfather asked the universe in his slightly raspy voice. "What to do?" The phrase would always be said twice, and from my perch on the bunk bed in the boys' room I knew he didn't expect an answer. But I always wondered, was this a general or a specific question? Was he asking about the entirety of his life, or was there something he needed to figure out? He never divulged.

He was pleased years later when I told him that my husband-to-be was named Mark. Before I married that apostle-named man, I phoned Grandfather to invite him to the wedding. He and Granny were living in a little apartment attached to Auntie Lou's house in Kingston, and I had gone there a few times to stay with them when Auntie Lou and Uncle Arthur had to take a trip somewhere. Grandfather was in his early nineties by then, but he continued to be the stoic, careful man I always knew. He often spoke of how, at this time in his life, he wished he could go off and live alone, like a hermit. It seemed strange, in his old age, that he would muse about giving up the family who were a constant throughout his life.

But once again Grandfather was speaking to the universe, and his quest appealed to me. He never accomplished this goal, but he was onto something: his wish was a version of the final stage of life described in Hindu teachings, when one becomes a *sanyasa* or renunciate, leaving worldly activity for spiritual development. I could easily imagine him, a skinny old man with a white fringe around his head, wearing simple robes and eating fruits and nuts in the forest, having renounced the material world for peace and spirituality.

I had sent Granny and Grandfather their wedding invitation, yet for some reason I needed to tell him in person that I wanted him there. "I can't make it," he said. "I'm not well." And I told him something I never had before, coming from a family that sidestepped deep issues, and because it had never felt necessary. "I love you, Grandfather," I said. "I know," he replied.

The morning after my wedding, with all the family assembled in Montreal, we got a call from Kingston to say that Grandfather had suffered a mild heart attack. He lived on for another year and never wavered in his faith. In hospital, dying of heart failure, he told his daughters that he was tired and ready to go, to meet his Maker.

chapter 4

brothers and sisters

EVEN AMONG THE PORTUGUESE CATHOLICS OF BRITISH GUIANA, ten children meant a large family. They were born in two groups of five, the constancy of childbirth interrupted for a few years because Granny suffered several miscarriages. I learned this when I was much older, and it dawned on me that she must have been pregnant or trying to be for more than twenty years. No wonder she had to hold everything together with that massive girdle.

The family unit always stayed tight, even when the siblings began to emigrate or brought marriage partners into the fold. Life gravitated around Granny and Grandfather. They might have resettled in Canada, but visits to Mother and Daddy with spouses and children continued to be commonplace. They often took holidays together.

From my earliest memories, the aunts and uncles I grew up with — Clement and Elaine, Lou and Arthur, Olga and Mike,

Uncle Charlie for a few years — along with Granny and Grandfather were the fabric of my young life. Some were boisterous, others quiet; most were kind and funny. They formed a whole cloth that enveloped me, cozy and comforting. I would sit at the dining table listening to them talk, or wander by as they proceeded through their days. I knew I needed them to be there, this lot of healthy, lively people, always busy, chatting, good-humoured, implicitly inclusive. They were adults, but I always thought of them as young.

Like many immigrants, when one family member got to the other side and pronounced it pretty good, in this case Uncle Steve to Canada, the rest followed one by one. Only when I began living in Canada did I wonder why the siblings would give up warm weather and a comfortable life for an unknown country, not realizing they were for the most part outrunning an uncertain future. "There was no opportunity there," my mother told me once, although I know she just needed to get away from the memories.

Gwendoline Dorothy Gomes grew up in a small house on Croal Street, just a few blocks away from the large home where I spent my childhood. She was a teenager by the time her family moved to 46 Brickdam. Along with her sisters, she went to St. Rose's High School, wearing those navy blue uniforms that I admired so much, riding her bicycle each day to and from school.

The eldest girl, she seemed to be a quiet force, not particularly shy but not boisterous either. She was considered steady and

My mother Gwen, far right, in a formal photo with her siblings. From left: Thelma, Clement, Lucille and Frank.

A bike ride in the Botanical Gardens. From left: Lucille, sister-in-law Elaine and my mother.

Right: My mother and father in the Botanical Gardens. August, 1945.

Opposite: Gwen and George posing on the Cricket Grounds.

Gwen photographed by my father at 46 Brickdam, the house where I grew up.

George in Trinidad.

My father's family. Aunt Gloria as a teenager with her half-sister Nina and her mother Ena, my grandmother.

Opposite, left: George on his tricycle. Paris, 1927.

Opposite, right: My grandfather Joseph Nebenzahl in South America. In his album, my father wrote: "Daddy, Mummy, Uncles Jules, Aunt Evelyn."

Below: One-year-old George at the beach with his mother Ena, right. Monte Carlo, 1926.

Left: Walking with Grandfather outside the house on Brickdam.

Opposite: At the photo studio in Georgetown with my mother. She is soon to leave for Canada.

With my brother George, near Granny's rose arbour in front of the house.

Saturday afternoon gathering of Grandfather's friends. Sir Donald Jackson is in the centre of the photo; Mr. Morris Fernandes in the foreground.

With my cousin Roslyn at Auntie Olga's wedding. Granny sits at the far right of the couch opposite.

Aunties Olga and Lucille at Wales, the sugar estate where we children spent our holidays.

Surrounded by family. From left: Auntie Thelma, me, baby George with our mother, Auntie Elaine and Auntie Olga.

kind-hearted, and her younger sisters spoke of her with respect and love; she would rarely squabble, which they often did. In the photographs taken before she married, I see a slender young woman with a confident look in her dark eyes. She was full of smiles in those early gatherings, but the camera would occasionally capture her in a quiet moment, as though she had other things on her mind besides having fun.

She didn't grow up with that many brothers and sisters without being the victim of childish disregard. Once, during a game of hide and seek, her brother Clement thought it would be fun to lock her in a trunk. "Here's a good place to hide," he told her, then closed the lid and ran off with his siblings. She panicked, banging and screaming, and for the rest of her life had a terror of enclosed spaces. "I'm claustrophobic," she would say to explain her anxiety in an elevator.

One summer when we lived in Canada, she became distraught on an afternoon drive near Niagara-on-the-Lake when a heavy fog set in. She began to feel it again, enclosed, stifled, and her anxiety attack only ended when my stepfather, in a stern voice that I had never heard before, told her to pull herself together. The fear and panic in her voice, the wild look in her eyes made me realize, despite my teenage disdain for her near hysteria, the power of the feelings that enveloped her.

My mother had been plagued with bouts of malaria from childhood, likely infected when she went to the countryside to visit her beloved grandmother. She would sometimes spend weeks in bed, sweating with fever or shivering so much that her teeth chattered. It came and went several times, she said, felling her with blinding headaches. This was before the prescription medication now used against the illness, so she was treated with quinine. Only after several courses of treatment did the symptoms disappear; she was never affected for the rest of her life.

Huge dark eyes peering out of a thin face, straight black hair cut into a bob, by all accounts she was not a troublemaker or a difficult child, but she was the first girl to face the challenges of growing up in a strict Portuguese household and was admired by her brothers and sisters for her peacemaking skills. In one photograph, she is around eight years old, standing with Clement beside a white wicker stroller that held her baby brother Stanley, her short dress revealing skinny legs and the same knobby knees that I developed at that age.

She seemed to enjoy going to school and was part of a boisterous group of friends at the tennis club and the swimming pool. But she had already experienced heartache by the time she met my father. She spoke little of the young man to whom she had been engaged, although she kept up a friendship with his parents and sister for the rest of her life. His name was Richard Amory, he lived with his parents in British Guiana and he had joined the Royal Air Force Volunteer Reserve. A navigator on a Lancaster bomber, he was only two or three flights away from the end of his service, homebound after a sortie to bomb railway facilities in tactical support of the Normandy invasion when the plane emerged from low cloud and crashed. He was twenty-two, and this was likely her first love. She kept photographs of him but never described his character to me or told me why she wanted to marry him. Or spoke of the feelings of loss she must have suffered when he died in July 1944.

My father was introduced to her at that same Brown Betty's I loved so much. "She had gone there with a friend who knew George and the friend introduced them," Auntie Lou said. "Boze, that's what everyone called him. He was a good-looking man, hear, very handsome." My mother spoke so little of him when I was growing up in Canada that I never knew whether their meeting was an aha! moment or whether it was a friendship that blossomed.

I'm betting on the former. You could see from the photographs they were physically attracted to each other — both young and fit and beautiful, a glowing couple, always touching or hugging or leaning into each other. They seem deeply happy. Then, when he found work in Trinidad, she argued with her father, loud arguments in which she held her ground — she was going to move there to be near him, even before they married. She was usually easygoing, but in this case she would not relent. Her siblings were awed by her courage.

It was a small wedding and only Uncle Clement, Granny and Auntie Lou, who was maid of honour, sailed to Port of Spain to attend. No Grandfather to walk his daughter down the aisle; he was laid up, apparently, after dental surgery. And no photographic record, even, of the church or reception; the only photo in my possession is posed outside the church showing my mother in a demure, close-fitting lace dress with long sleeves, holding a bouquet of daisies and greenery, two bunches of flowers behind her ears attached to her trailing veil. Auntie Lou, wearing a large picture hat and ruffled floor-length dress, is carrying such a large bouquet it looks like she's getting married too. Granny, in a dark belted dress with handbag and gloves, stands beside Uncle Clement, dapper in a double-breasted dark suit. Such sombre clothes to wear at a wedding.

My mother is smiling but my father, in a single-breasted summer suit with a rose in his lapel, is not. He was manager of a large bakery in Port of Spain, and seems thinner than in his earlier photos, his moustache making his face look even leaner. They were married for about eighteen months, and I want to imagine that their tiny house in Port of Spain was full of love and sex and happiness. I was born four months before his death, and I treasure the one photo he might have taken of me, a chubby, smiling baby standing in a crib. "Your father was so happy with you," my mother said more than once, many years later. "He marvelled at your little fingers, your tiny, perfect ears."

Would my parents have stayed in Trinidad? My mother was already pregnant with my brother just a few months after my birth. Would they have had more children? Those decisions were taken out of their hands. At the house on Brickdam Street, the call came to the next-door neighbour, Mr. Lee, who had a phone. My father was dead.

This time it was Grandfather who went to Port of Spain, and father and daughter buried her young husband in Woodbrook Cemetery, in a pebble-strewn plot surrounded by a small concrete wall. I have a black and white photo — did she take it? — showing the plot, a glass bowl of flowers where there should have been a headstone. I found in her papers several forms she filled out for "Grant of Exclusive Right of Burial at Woodbrook Cemetery, Port of Spain" for a payment of twenty-four dollars. The forms are dated March 1950, and give her in perpetuity a plot for burial that I assume is right beside my father's.

My mother returned to Georgetown with me, her baby girl, her belly just beginning to swell with their second child. When I picture that journey, I'm reminded of the famous photo of Jackie Kennedy in the bloodstained watermelon-pink suit, taken after her husband's assassination, her face dull with shock and pain, unable to comprehend her loss. So it must have been for my mother and after three years, through the fog of her grief, she made her way to join her brothers and sisters in Canada. She was seeking a life, I'm guessing, that didn't remind her constantly of my father.

She rarely mentioned what it felt like being a mother in those few years before she left. She did talk about giving birth to my brother, drinking a concoction called Twilight Sleep which was known to make you happily semi-conscious. I can imagine, months after her husband's death, the loneliness and stress, mixed with the happiness of giving birth to a healthy son. She must have wept, holding that baby boy in her arms.

And me. She mentioned more than once how she liked to bathe me and dress me so that the nanny, Louisa, could take me out for a walk in the stroller. And she enjoyed telling the story of how she rescued me at the house on Brickdam Street, when I had somehow climbed unnoticed through the casement window onto the corrugated metal roof separating the girls' room and the tower — a dangerous spot, considering a fall off that roof meant landing two storeys down in Granny's arbour, or on the concrete drive. No one dared go out after me in case I ran to the edge, so the adults stood at the window calling me, panicking. But I refused to budge, my mother said. "Then I put my hand behind my back and said softly, 'Donna, I've got some candy for you. Come here and see.' And you ran into my arms."

How did she leave us, I wonder? Ships sailing to Canada from Georgetown often departed in the early evening. Did she put us to bed, knowing all the while that it would be the last time? Or did she leave earlier, saying goodbye with a jaunty wave, telling us she would be back soon? Did she steal a last look at our sleeping forms or touch our heads, put her lips against our downy cheeks, then go to the car to be driven to the waiting ship?

Decades later, when I became a mother and so in love with my babies, I was nearly felled when I realized what she had done.

◇

The oldest sibling, Clement, and his wife Elaine, who was born in Dutch Guiana, were the last of the family to leave the country. I never knew the depth of Uncle Clement's relationship with my grandfather, but he was always nearby, living close and on call if his parents needed him. Clem, as he was known, took up the retail trade just like his father, employed first at Bettencourt's when I was growing up, then managing a branch of the Trinidad-based distribution company T. Geddes Grant, after Granny and Grandfather had gone to Canada. It must have been a great support for my grandparents, with their strong tradition of family ties, that Uncle Clement and his family had not joined the Portuguese who were emigrating in droves starting in the 1950s.

A tall man with wavy brown hair who usually wore short-sleeve shirts and khaki pants, Uncle Clement sported a lovely brush moustache. His great passion was the Sea Scouts and although I never understood what it meant to be a Sea Scout leader, except that it had a lot to do with water and nautical clothing, I knew that he was an important man in those circles. Maybe running the Scouts gave him the skills to handle difficulties without blinking, because I never saw Uncle lose his cool.

Friendly in a quiet way, he dedicated his free time to sailing and scouting. The room under his small home was filled with Scout gear and papers, the site of his officers' meetings — no children allowed. The Scout leader and his minions, discussing important matters, never noticed that Roslyn and her siblings would sometimes listen in through a crack in their bedroom floorboard. Uncle's capability was recognized, too, because during my childhood he had been named Sea Scout leader for the entire country. He had even, we were told, met Princess Margaret.

We younger children never went out on the sleek Scout sailboat the Roslyn Ann, named after my cousin, although both Roslyn and her brother Paul were considered old enough to be taken sailing occasionally, much to our silent envy. But we did benefit from the Scouts in other ways. At some point they had acquired a series of low, concrete-block bungalows at the edge of the jungle that made up three-quarters of British Guiana. The country, bordering Brazil, Venezuela and Dutch Guiana, holds one of the largest expanses of untouched rainforest in the world. Known as "the Base," this spot, abandoned by U.S. forces after the Second World War, was the Scouts' centre for jungle expeditions.

This is where we are headed one hot Sunday morning, Scouts and children in a couple of Uncle Clement's Scout jeeps. It feels like we're no sooner out of the city than we turn toward the treeline, bumping along dusty, rutted roads. Hanging on in the metal-framed jeep, all I'm seeing as we enter the jungle are tree trunks, limbs and vines. Finally we reach a clearing where three squat grey buildings stand in a semicircle: the Scouts' jungle HQ, the famous Base.

For me, it is a wonderland. Light filters through the rainforest canopy; the air smells green, of damp earth and foliage. The jungle, the subject of Granny's scary stories, is all around me, except there's nothing to fear, because the brave Scouts are here too, with Uncle Clement at the lead. And this trip, made in those tough, four-wheel-drive jeeps, is not a naturalist's excursion to observe the forested canopy, nor is it survival training in a jungle setting. Just around a bend lies the purpose of today's outing: the particular pleasure of swimming in Red Water Creek.

Because of minerals in the soil, the water that flows along the meandering creek and into the basin where we are going to swim is a deep red, yet so clear that you can see down to the rippling sandy bottom. We follow the stream until it opens into the large pool, which in the sunshine sparkles as though a thousand diamonds are bouncing off its surface. The adults immediately strip down to bathing trunks, the daring ones cannonballing into the pool with mighty splashes. As I step carefully into the cool water, I'm buoyed by their high spirits, surrounded by their laughter. Thrilled to be a part of it, I've managed to forget that this is the only time I have ever been swimming. No one, including me, seems to consider that I can't swim, or that the bottom of a natural pool can have unexpected dips and ridges.

I am a careful child: no leaping or rushing into the water like my high-spirited cousins. The sun warms my shoulders, the sand feels roughly tender underfoot. I walk slowly, yet I take only a few steps into the basin when I lose my footing. The sandy bottom suddenly slips away, my knees buckle, and soon

I'm under water. I have no idea what to do; it's so sparkling in the red water that I'm mesmerized even as I go under. The next thing I know I'm being scooped up, sputtering and coughing, by Uncle Clement who casually slings me on his shoulder and deposits me back in shallow water. The incident will never be discussed, and I know well enough not to tell Granny and Grandfather about it. I also learn, as soon as the opportunity presents itself, how to swim.

I survive that first near-death experience only to face a second, again with Uncle Clement leading the way. One afternoon, George and I and our older cousin Paul are taking a drive with him when suddenly Uncle pulls in at the dockyards. This comes as a surprise to us, although I realize later that it was the point of the drive. We must stop for a bit, Uncle says, so that he can check on the Roslyn Ann, the Sea Scout's schooner, which is docked just beyond these buildings. He parks the car in the middle of what feels like a large expanse of packed dirt surrounded by unpainted wooden sheds. "You'll be fine. Just stay in the car," he tells us.

I'm sure Uncle feels that staying in a solitary car surrounded by gloomy, ramshackle buildings isn't dangerous, but we are three children with childish imaginations, scared to be alone and quietly panicking. At first, anyways. The sky is getting darker by the moment and the empty windows that encircle us feel threatening. My heart is beating hard, and as the sun slants further down the horizon and the shadows grow longer, we are so frightened that we're near tears. Finally I just can't take it. "I'm going to find Uncle," I declare, trying to sound brave. "No, no!" the boys scream. "He said we had to stay here!"

It's a pivotal moment for me: should I stay in the car, doing nothing except feeling terrified, or should I go and find him, no matter how scary a prospect that is? I feel compelled to take my chances — better to do something than nothing — so I open the car door and step outside, the boys' pleas echoing behind me. Maybe I'm forced into bravery by their panicked tears, but once I'm outside the car, I realize, scanning the murky yard, that I don't know where Uncle has gone. I can vaguely see, through an opening between the buildings, the dock where the boats are berthed, but my bad eyesight hasn't been detected yet and so it's all a dark haze to me. I plod on, knowing that he's on a boat somewhere, and find my way to a long jetty made of planks that seem to be carpeted with large holes. The tide is out because, looking way down, I can see in the glistening darkness a sea of deep mud.

Inching forward, leaking tears, so terrified that I'm going to miss my footing and plunge into the mud that I'm about to crouch on hands and knees and crawl, I am suddenly lifted up by one of the Sea Scout cadets, who carries me to the boat. I recount my story of panic to a bemused Uncle Clement who, cool as ever, shepherds me back to the car.

Still sniffling, I return to the wide-eyed boys in the back seat. I feel quietly proud, like I had somehow triumphed over adversity. Yet for years afterward, I would occasionally dream of being imprisoned in a large square surrounded by dark sheds, walking backward in fear, trying to avoid my captors.

Two aunts were another constant in my early life: Lucille, the careful, well-organized aunt who married Arthur, a Scotsman with aquiline features and sandy hair that flopped over his eyes; and Olga, the rebel youngest daughter who was just eighteen when she married Uncle Mike, the handsome Englishman. I was six at the time, so until she left for Canada three years later, she was, next to Granny, my closest mother figure.

Auntie Olga had a lot of spunk and sometimes got herself into trouble. Once, when she was ferrying me back from school for lunch on the back of her bike, I managed to get my foot caught in the spokes of the back wheel as I tried to dismount. Twisted ankle, much wailing, and she was told off by my grandparents for not caring properly for me. She was kind-hearted but could be dangerously strong-willed. I bore the brunt of that one day when a woman friend of the family, young and married, suggested she would take me to visit Uncle Arthur, who was in hospital. I was excited to go, put on a dress, brushed my hair, but Auntie Olga decided this young woman was inappropriately interested in my uncle and was taking me just so she could spend time with him. I became a pawn in Olga's attempt to foil this plot when she insisted that I couldn't go because, well, I needed a haircut. To prove her point, she sat me down on a dining-room chair with a towel around my shoulders and grimly proceeded, snipping away, ringlets flying, to make a mess of my pretty curly hair. She got her way; the visit was called off and I spent what felt like hours sobbing from behind an armchair in the living room as Auntie Olga tried to explain, without telling the truth, why my hair had been sacrificed for her mission.

Olga spent a lot of time acting out and testing boundaries with Grandfather, who was a strict parent. She rarely won those battles. In bed in the girls' room that I shared with Auntie Olga, I was startled out of my sleep one night by the sound of Grandfather, standing above the bed, hitting her with his belt because she had come in late from a dance. It was acceptable then for a parent to slap a child, but it happened rarely in our house, so to witness that level of violence and pain frightened me. The next day, no one spoke about it, and I looked over at Grandfather, wondering how he could be so cruel to Auntie Olga. This was before she married; once she had been deposited by another man's side, Grandfather no longer had that kind of power over her.

When Olga got married, Roslyn and I decided we were going to be included in every photograph taken by the official photographer. Just like Auntie Lou's wedding the year before, Auntie Olga's wedding reception took place in the expansive living rooms at the house, so we knew the lay of the land. But it wasn't easy; we couldn't let the photographer out of our sight, and we had to plant ourselves in the photos without being obvious and then being told to go away. You can still see us there, both dressed in plaid pinafores, Roslyn's hair in ringlets, peering around from the edge of a couch or through the bodies of a group or even right behind the bride and groom. We still declare the experience a great success.

But while Auntie Olga was exuberant, Auntie Lou was more circumspect. It showed up in how carefully she dressed and how fastidious she was in her housekeeping. I see her in the classic shirtwaist dresses she favoured, often turned out in high heels. She must have liked those because she and Uncle Arthur, years later in Canada, took up ballroom dancing; Lou got to wear more glittery versions of the dresses and high heels she liked, while being twirled across the floor. She was a mystery to me, always responsible and kind, sometimes very funny, but I never felt I understood her. She kept that real self well guarded.

I didn't know most of my uncles when I was growing up. Clement was there, of course, and Charlie with his motorcycle friends. Uncle Charlie loved cars: he could fix anything mechanical and he was an artist, those big toolmaker's hands fashioning beautiful metal sculptures. He was a gentle, kind-hearted soul who spoke quietly and never lost his temper, the first of the brothers to die, of a brain tumour, just in his fifties.

Uncle Frank was dapper, always well turned out in a jacket and tie, the tallest of the brothers, most of whom carried the Portuguese build, short and a bit heavy-set. Never without a pencil-thin moustache, he was renowned in the family because he had once been an extra in a Harry Belafonte movie set in Barbados.

Then there was Uncle Steve, the one who was sent away to sea at sixteen, accidentally he claimed. In his telling, Charlie was supposed to go to sea, but he was Granny's favourite and at the last minute she convinced Grandfather that Steve would be better suited for a marine life. Turns out she was right.

I basked in the pleasure of being around as my aunts and uncles chatted and laughed. After we moved to Canada, even when they became parents and added their own little children to the scene, there would come a point at any family gathering when they began to talk about their escapades while they lived at home with Mother and Daddy. The Caribbean lilt that had grown muted over the years would become more pronounced, along with the Guyanese expressions. "Come, nuh, chile," one of the aunties would say to force an agreement with her point.

They would reminisce about Cookie's pepperpot and Granny's black cake, the time Steve was found sleepwalking his way through an open window in their house on Croal Street, or when Clement jauntily led the Sea Scouts on a march through Georgetown to mark the visit by Princess Margaret and, heading the troop up our street, saluted smartly when he passed the house. They would remember when Lou had her first child and the phone call came to our neighbour to let us know before Grandfather had even returned from taking her to the hospital. I felt a deep sense of connection to know that these stories were my past, layered as they were with the nostalgia of having left that beautiful, nurturing place.

How could she have left us? I asked myself that question for years, and I'm ashamed that I only looked at it from my own perspective, the abandoned child. Then, in therapy and a mother for the first time, I was jarred by the hot anger I felt toward my mother. I finally asked her. And even though she could be so temperamental around the men who cared for her, my brother and stepfather, when she responded her tone was measured, quiet. She didn't waver, and I could see the strength in her that her sisters so admired. "I did what I thought would be best for you and George," she said. "You have no idea how many nights I cried myself to sleep."

My mother returned to Georgetown when my brother was ill with nephritis. It must have been hard for her to take time off from her secretarial job in Montreal and fly back to British Guiana. I was excited, full of bubbles inside to see this person I didn't know, my mother who loved me. But I remember the meeting, when I got home from school, being not effusive or fraught with feeling but curiously flat. I felt shy and quite unhappy that a day earlier, while I was playing in Granny's rose arbour, something had stung my eyelid which had puffed up alarmingly.

I can't imagine what it must have been like to see your children for the first time in years, to realize the time you missed, especially when one of them is worryingly ill. I was unconcerned about George's illness; I never doubted he would be all right. But how did she feel, seeing her little boy, his dark hair and hazel eyes the image of her lost husband? She seemed calm, reserved, and I thought her sophisticated and beautiful with her short black hair, straight nose and lovely arched brows, her high cheekbones and deep brown eyes. But those dark eyes held something that I didn't understand at the time.

She must have stayed a few weeks; photographs show that she spent time at Wales with her married sisters. But I have no sense of time, just that she went away. And even though I remember her arrival, I cannot conjure up her departure. Did she leave when I was at school, and when I returned my ongoing life just swallowed up her absence? Did we say goodbye, were tears shed? I can imagine my mother holding back, not wanting to share her sadness with us. While she might have spent a long time at George's bedside, for me it was as though she just appeared in my life and before I had a chance to feel like she was part of my world, she was gone. I don't recall either sadness about her departure or anticipation about seeing her again.

George and I lived without her for seven years. In that time we sailed to Canada once for a few months and she visited once: the sum total of our encounters except for those early, misty years of babyhood. There was never a phone at the house, so she kept in contact with cards and letters, although if she wrote with any regularity, only Granny knew. My mother was never one to wear her deep feelings on her sleeve, and as I grew older I realized that she was almost childlike in her ability to anger quickly, and to forget. She rarely talked about her past, as though it was a door she had locked and couldn't bring herself to reopen, except in her own thoughts and dreams.

Then one day in her elder years, in Canada, she took me to the dresser drawer in her bedroom and showed me, tucked into a tiny cloth bag, a pair of small white lace-up boots. For all those years, she had kept my baby shoes.

part two

Footfalls echo in the memory
Down the passage which we did not take
Towards the door we never opened
Into the rose garden.

— T.S. Eliot, "Burnt Norton" from *Four Quartets*

chapter 5

out of the shadows

I KNOW SO MUCH ABOUT MY MOTHER'S STORY, IT'S LIKE BREATHING. I inhale and my aunts are talking about the tennis club and the cricket team, Granny's buldamel and Grandfather's bedtime rituals. I exhale and there are my Portuguese great-grandmothers with their dark dresses, their round bodies and delicious coffee. Another breath and I'm sitting on Granny's lap in the tower, my life unfolding in this tropical city with its Atlantic breezes and monsoon rains.

Until we left for Canada, I was surrounded by my mother's family. They were essential to those stories of warm nights under mosquito nets and walks along the Sea Wall, school days in my blue gingham dress and the lively crowd around the dining table, presided over by Grandfather with his crown of hair. I knew little about the lives of my hard-working Madeiran ancestors, but I inhaled the tropical air they had breathed and walked the streets where they had walked. All those generations formed and supported me, like each breath I took.

My father's story, on the other hand, is in shadow. He was gone, invisible to me, the little I knew of him just a few sketches made by family members during my early years, fading quickly. I don't know whether the family wanted my mother to be the one to talk about my father and so refrained, or whether they really didn't know much. And by the time I was old enough to ask questions, there was no one to bring these stories into the light. The people who were connected to Georges Louis Paul Nebenzahl, the man who hovered like a ghost in my head throughout my life, had disappeared even before I could speak.

Because he was born in a place where his parents were not citizens, my father had scant evidence of his nationality. My mother had kept several of his documents, each described as a Certificate of Identity: long pages, in English and French, with stamps of British Guiana showing the picture of King George VI, my father's snapshot in the upper left corner. He's only nineteen in the first, listed as Document 4, issued in September 1944 and valid for one year. It offers the following details:

```
Height: 5'10½"
Hair: Black
Date of Birth: 29 April 1925
Place of Birth: Monte Carlo, Monaco
Nationality of Origin: Belgium
Former residence abroad: Paris
```

It's signed with a clear, strong signature, and he's obviously anglicized now, using the first name George without the S. it seems likely he has been using these documents since he arrived in British Guiana. Why, since his mother is a British citizen? Were his birthplace and father's origin the reason?

It's possible he was planning on travelling but had no passport — the certificate is to be used, it states, "in lieu of a national passport." In the photo attached to a corner of the second document, he has a moustache and looks much thinner. This one is issued in Trinidad in September 1948, and the copy I have is without any stamps; he is not yet married but soon will be. In both documents his father is named Joseph Nebenzahl, but his mother's name has changed: Frances Ena Hart, once Ena Nebenzahl, has become Ena Spratt. She has married again.

I know my father from the pages of his photo album. This carefully assembled, cloth-covered album speaks to a fastidious man with a sentimental nature, who captioned in black ink with a meticulous hand the photographs on its faded green pages. Framed with black triangular corners, snapshots of family and many friends fill the book: captured moments in the lives of laughing groups of young people gathered to play outdoors, in bathing suits or cricket whites. He is here, lean body, curly hair, often at the front of a group, mugging for the camera, laughing with his buddies. He looks like someone with a sense of humour. Or the comedian, covering up his sadness with a joke.

At the front of his album are several pages of childhood pictures, most of them raising as many questions as they might answer. Family photos, taken in Europe in the 1920s, in a world recovering from the Great War, unaware of the devastation soon to be unleashed. The one that captivates me most is almost surreal in its composition. Sepia-toned, it shows in the bottom right corner a slender young woman in a one-piece maillot crouched on an expanse of sand. Her hair is cut in a short bob, popular in the period, and her gaze is focused on a chubby toddler in the left foreground in what looks like a matching one-piece swimsuit, a serious, round-faced little boy with a mop of dark curls. There's a mound at her knees, a roughly built sandcastle, and although the child is reaching for a large stick planted in the sand near his right hand, his full attention is on the camera.

Behind him, a portly man in a suit and a homburg sits upright on a folding beach chair, squinting into the middle distance, his elbows bent, hands resting on his thighs. Farther back, slightly out of focus in the centre of the photo, three men and a woman are standing at the water's edge, the men in dark pants and jackets with V-necked vests and collarless white shirts, each wearing a brimmed cap, the woman in a dark cloche hat and drop-waisted dress. Across the water behind them, a long boardwalk or causeway traverses the scene. The carefully written caption reads: "Monte Carlo, 1926."

My father was born in 1925, so when this photograph was taken, he was just a year old. I wonder, is she so attentive because he has just learned how to walk, and he's taking early steps? And who is the man in the suit? Could he be a relative, or is he just someone taking the sea air when my chubby father wanders across the sand and the photographer presses the shutter? Is the child's attention so riveted because his own father is holding the camera?

At the bottom of the page, its edges fading to brown, the same little boy appears in a photo captioned "Paris, 1927." He looks happy, riding in a gravel courtyard on the saddle of a pony tricycle with oversize metal wheels, the handlebars extending from just above its ears. The weather must be cool, since he's dressed in pale knit pants and a buttoned sweater, wearing little leather shoes and a fuzzy hat, his wide smile reaching his eyes. The background shows two sets of stone steps leading to plain inset doors, austere, like the back of a building. There's crumbling stone beside one doorway, a rectangular stained-glass window on the other side and what looks like a sculpted support, possibly for a light. Against this slightly forbidding backdrop, the boy smiles easily at the camera, a wisp of dark hair showing below the knit cap. He is two years old.

The third photo is tagged in large letters, "Paris — 1928." Now the three-year-old, in long-sleeved cotton pyjamas with a high collar, wearing slippers with a furry trim, climbs up some wide granite steps, a high stone balustrade on his left supported by stone columns. Part of one of the front windows is in view, tall double windows with wooden shutters, open, and a small wrought-iron Juliet balcony across the lower portion. One foot rests on the step above as the boy turns toward the camera, carrying a plate at such an angle that whatever was on it has likely fallen to the ground. Was he returning from breakfasting outdoors? Was he going to visit a friend or family member? No smile this time but his lips are slightly turned up and, once again, there's a level gaze from those clear hazel eyes.

Not long after these photos were taken, little George and his parents set sail for British Guiana where his maternal grandparents, of Welsh and Irish descent, were among the small percentage of British in the colony who were not part of the ruling class. His sister Gloria, four years younger, was born in July 1929 in Georgetown. The birth certificate lists her parents as Ena and Joseph Nebenzahl.

On another of the thick pages, softened with age and pulled away from the rings that held them, a photo has been cut out and I can find no match in my mother's collections. The smaller of the two remaining pictures shows a skinny boy at the front gate of a tropical house, wearing white tennis shoes and long shorts. He's in a boxing stance: elbows bent, gloved hands clenched near his face. The caption, in black ink, again in writing clear and straight, says "Self at 8 years," meaning it's now 1933. The fence, of unpainted wood, and the gate with chicken wire filling its frame show a simple entry, the back gate perhaps, although the louvred windows on the upper floor and the carved support column look more genteel.

In the other photograph, four people dressed in white are posed on the outdoor staircase of a house with lovely, rounded columns at top and bottom, a carved balustrade enclosing them, louvred windows above. A dark waxy-leafed bush dotted with pale, lily-shaped flowers cascades alongside the seated quartet. They look happy, full of life, at ease in front of the camera.

Since I first saw this photo as a child, I have been riveted by two of these people: the man at the top with a narrow, handsome face and hooded eyes, straight dark hair combed back, whose right arm reaches over the shoulder of the woman seated below him, his fingers entwined in hers. She wears a long string of white beads and her hair curls around her forehead; her lips curve slightly. Her eyes hold the camera. I can see my father's face in that gaze, the hazel eyes and bow lips.

In his careful script, my father has written in capital letters: Daddy, Mummy, Uncle Jules, Aunt Evelyn. This is the only photographic record of my father's father, my grandfather Joseph. Who knows what secrets that missing photo might have divulged?

For years, because I had been told that Joseph had not returned with his wife and child to British Guiana, I believed this photo was taken somewhere near Monte Carlo. Then one day it dawned on me that the part of the building in the photograph was identical to the house in the snapshot of my father in boxing gloves, taken in B.G. I was so convinced that my grandfather had stayed in Europe, I glossed over the outdoor stairs and louvred windows. This was the same place. Joseph Nebenzahl must have settled in Georgetown with his wife and children, for at least those four years.

There are no records or reminiscences of this period, of the work he did or the house where they lived. But for the first time, I saw the connection between the two photos. There, I imagine, stood my grandfather, photographing his son as he posed in his boxing gloves. There stood my eight-year-old father, at the bottom of the front steps that he climbed regularly, taking a photo of his mother and father, aunt and uncle, making them smile.

My grandfather was there in Georgetown, in 1933; I never discovered more about Uncle Jules and Aunt Evelyn, except that she, possibly, was my grandmother's sister. But I do know that Joseph and Ena went back to Europe, sometime after 1933, when Hitler had just become chancellor of Germany and the continent had begun the countdown toward war. The Nebenzahl story has begun to fade away.

After his parents left for Europe, what was life like for George? The early photos show good cheer, which is hard to manufacture in a child, so I imagine that he was happy growing up in Monte Carlo and Paris. Then he spent important, formative years in South America with his mother, his father and his little sister Gloria. How could he help but feel deserted when his parents left?

When I was older, I began to see the similarity in this chronicle of abandonment. George and Gloria were left behind and, decades later, Donna and George were left behind. But there was one huge difference: our extended families. My aunts mentioned several times that Ena's parents, in whose house George and Gloria were sent to live, were not doting grandparents. "The grandad was an angry man," Auntie Lou said, "very crabby. And she was very meek. It couldn't have been a happy time for those kids."

Joseph and Ena didn't fare well either. I found her name in the manifest of the SS Champlain sailing from Le Havre in France to New York City in January 1934. She described herself as Ena Nebenzahl, married, a citizen of Belgium with a home address in Paris. She indicated she would be in New York for two months, staying at a hotel facing Lincoln Square in an area known as San Juan Hill, home to thousands of African-American and Caribbean families, famed for jazz and art; it was razed in the late 1940s to make way for Lincoln Center.

She never returned to Joseph. By 1937 she had married a man named Serge Abagoff, claiming on the marriage certificate that he was her first husband. As a child, I was told that he was a White Russian count, and I visualized a bearded man wearing tall boots and a fur hat. But in fact, Abagoff was a modern dancer in New York, his name mentioned a few times in *Billboard* magazine during the 1930s.

That marriage was not a success, either. By around 1938, Ena had left Abagoff and returned to British Guiana, this time with a baby daughter named Nina in her arms. The two children in

South America, waiting for their parents' return, instead greeted their mother and a child who was a stranger to them.

So in the space of about five years, Ena had discarded two husbands. How did her young son feel when he realized that he might never see his father again?

Once he was in his late teens, my father began recording his own story, on display in that album. I see a young man surrounded by friends; he has a slight build, an expressive face, a cigarette sometimes appearing between his fingers or his lips. He's smiling and playing around a lot, and from time to time the photos capture that level gaze, those hazel eyes.

There is a section titled Family, in which his mother and sisters appear. Photos of Gloria show her as a tall teenager holding hands with a little girl with straight brown hair, her half-sister Nina. Ena appears in other snapshots, looking older but still slender and pretty, her face crinkling in the sunshine.

Lots of photos, from the cricket club and the swimming pool, show laughing groups of young people, featuring tanned, active young women; one of them might be singled out for a page or two, posing for more formal photos. Then, near the back of the album, a young woman who has begun to appear in group photos takes centre stage. On page after page, each one inscribed "Gwen Gomes" at the top in his careful writing, he photographs her. There she is, posed in profile on a cement platform near a swimming pool, wearing a demure two-piece bathing suit; looking sultry among tall grasses in white shorts and a cap-sleeved white shirt; in a dark dress with a white collar, wheeling her bike, smiling at the camera. She is my mother.

The photos become more intimate. In one labelled "Botanical Gardens, August 22, 1945," they're dressed up, going somewhere. He stands behind her in a white, short-sleeved shirt and white pants, arms around her middle; her hands cover his, he leans down so they are cheek to cheek. Her dark dress is softly pleated, a string of pearls encircles her neck; they both wear watches. They smile at the camera, close-mouthed, like they have a secret. Now it's September and they're in the water, hugging, or sitting on the grassy lawn of the cricket club, dressed like they're about to go for a swim, her legs in one direction and his in another, his arms close around her, their heads together, laughing for the camera. At the Wireless Station pool after a swim, her wet hair clinging to her back, he's on one knee, arms round her middle, and she's standing close to his body; their smiles are wide and loving.

Then a series of studies of my mother sitting, shoulder-length hair swept off her face, the front rolled up and under and pinned into place, a popular 1940s style known as a "victory roll." She looks, close-mouthed, at the camera, dark eyes, shapely brows, wearing red lipstick. In another page of photos, taken in my grandparents' house, her skin looks brown and smooth against white shorts and a white short-sleeved shirt with dark pearl buttons. She sits, legs drawn up on the Morris couch with its wide mahogany arms and pink patterned cushions that I remember so well. He is lying with his head on her lap. Her fingernails are painted dark red; they're laughing.

He's active, exuberant even, in many of the group photos. But the expression I always loved appears in a photo I carried with me for years, where he's perched on a wooden gate in front of a swimming pool, alone. He's in a bathing suit, leaning forward slightly to rest his elbows on his knees, cigarette between two fingers. He's got a slight smile on his lips but it's the gaze that holds you, that level gaze, those clear hazel eyes looking straight at the camera. Underneath that lively demeanor, my mother once told me, he was shy, a truth glimpsed only in those moments of calm.

These photos capture them falling in love, and they are shining, full of joy. What a difference from the photo of my mother taken just a few years later in her application for immigration to Canada. Her hair is cut, stylish, parted on the side with a kiss curl at her forehead. She's wearing dark lipstick; she looks at the camera. She is no longer smiling.

Although I spent many years ignoring it, my father's death was the tragedy of my life. I know that, although I don't feel it. Or is it that I feel it, but don't really know it?

How many times, as I turned the faded pages in that album and searched for his face, have I imagined his young life? I felt too unprotected emotionally to embrace the insight that he, too, had pored over these photographs. Yet I wanted to step into those pages, to feel the gravel underfoot in that Paris courtyard, to stand with the photographer capturing the eight-year-old with his boxing gloves. I wanted to smell the greenery in the Botanical Gardens as I watched him and my mother smile into each other's eyes.

First the toddler, then the eight-year-old, then the young man. But more than a young man, this smiling twenty-five-year-old was also a parent. "He deserved more," my Aunt Gloria once told me. In the photos he looks engaged, vital, so alive, even though he carried the insecurity of his upbringing, the loss of his father and his disappointment with his mother, who Gloria described as being wilful, neglectful.

I had always been hesitant to ask my aunts about him, afraid that they would say something negative or inconsequential, and I would be disappointed. When I finally asked, their comments were basic, mundane even. But I was hungry for every morsel.

Auntie Thelma left for Canada when I was about three and was part of the group in many of those photos of laughing young people. Yes, she knew my father, she told me. She found him outspoken and friendly. "He liked to talk — he was never shy about that," she said. "And he liked to be around people. I always found him to be nice."

I can spot Auntie Thelma, the first of the sisters to leave for Canada, in some of those snapshots. At that time, my father worked in the office of Pan American Airways, and he's photographed jauntily dressed in a short-sleeved white shirt with epaulets and white pants and a visored, flat-topped hat. He had lots of friends, Thelma said, lots of guys. "We used to go for picnics on Sunday in the backdam" — the name for rural, undeveloped land outside the town, possibly an area that had been dammed to prevent flooding. He lived on his own in a boarding house, she recalled, and became good friends with another boarder named Sonny Francis. A few years later, Sonny Francis became my godfather and was a great support to my mother when my father died. They remained lifelong friends; even after we came to Canada, he would send me gifts.

All the aunts agreed that George was very nice to look at. "He was a good-looking man, hear, a very handsome-looking man," said Auntie Lou. But she also described someone who was a bit odd, at least by her account. "He loved to eat bananas, except at night. And he would go to dances and never dance!"

"He was very handsome," Auntie Thelma agreed. "Lots of girls were after George." He was even noticed by the gossip writers for the local newspaper, my mother once said. "They called him Boze, that was his nickname, and they would write when he was playing cricket and what girl he was dating."

His mother, Ena, was so beautiful that once when she walked down the street in her big picture hat, people at the office where my mother worked leaned out the window to get a look. "Beautiful but not a good mother," said Auntie Lou, who recalled visiting a friend next door to the house when my father was still living with his mother and sisters. Because of the American airbase nearby, there were a lot of Americans around and she had a lot of parties, Lou said.

No question this behaviour affected her young son. "Your father disapproved of his own mother," my mother told me once.

Auntie Thelma, who was at Brown Betty's the first time my father and mother met, recalled that he had a very bad stomach. "He always used to tell your mom, 'Don't touch my stomach'," she said. And he was stubborn. "He wouldn't go to the hospital. He said he would feel better tomorrow."

The bits and pieces of information that I collected about my father showed a complex, even contradictory person, friendly and outgoing yet shy and careful. "Your father was a happy man," Auntie Lou assured me. Perhaps this was wishful thinking or an attempt to recreate for a fatherless child the vision of someone who would have brought sunshine, had he been there. I'm convinced that he must have felt loneliness in those early years without his own parents around. Unlike me, he knew what he was missing.

Nothing exerts a stronger effect on a child than the unlived life of a parent, Jungian philosophy contends. In her book on the effect of absent fathers on their daughters, Jungian analyst Susan E. Schwartz describes how a baby daughter will see herself reflected in her father's eyes, and that becomes a cue for her sense of self. An absent father – whether through neglect or abandonment – withholds that mirroring from his child, who then perceives herself as someone unable to claim a father's love. But I knew he loved me for those few short months, just like I knew that what happened to him, why he left us, was out of his control. And I didn't want to know more, at first anyway.

I never asked anyone how my father had died, so I can't recall where I heard the story about hiccups. Then one day my cousin Roslyn informed me that yes, my father had died of hiccups. The only way to prevent hiccups, she said solemnly, was to drink a glass of water that you stirred with a spoon. It seemed a whimsical, frightening way to die, although I never allowed myself to conjure up what death by hiccups could look like. I've had a muted anxiety about hiccups ever since.

"Your father loved to play with you," my mother once said. At the time of his death, I was no more than four months old, the laughing and rolling over stage. Babies at this age like to touch and smile, they like sounds and voices, so I hope we had happy times together. But I was there in that little house in Trinidad on the night he was dying, at least until my mother asked my godmother Marie to take me away.

What a nightmare it must have been. Everything seemed to conspire against him, even though he had a terrible pain in his gut that should have warned him. Did my mother keep hoping that the bleeding would stop? At what point did she realize, too late, that he wasn't going to make it? He started to feel ill on Friday after work and by Saturday he was dead. "Your mother had a nurse friend, but no one could talk him into going to the hospital," Auntie Olga said. The doctor was called the next morning, but apparently didn't show up until his golf game was over. "By then it was too late."

"A duodenal ulcer that hemorrhaged" is the description I use when people ask me how my father died. Simple words for a monumental loss. Did I feel that loss too? I remember nothing of my life until after my mother's departure for Canada. Everything before was a story that I was told or, all too frequently, not told.

We were under four years old, my brother and I, when she left. But at that age, children have emotional bonds, connections with the people they love. Surely, we were aware that she was gone? I never posed the question until years later, on a bright summer day at my mother and stepfather's farmstead near Uxbridge, Ontario. I was sitting with Auntie Olga and a couple of cousins in the shade of a large oak tree, enjoying the day, when I casually asked Olga if she remembered how I reacted. "Oh, when your mother left, you cried and cried," she said. "You ran around the house calling her name." I was shocked into silence. "But then you forgot about it," she added quickly. Her voice was cheery, but I sensed that she knew she had spoken about something that was never meant to be revealed.

Of course, I thought, I would have been heartbroken without my mother near me, despite the house overflowing with aunts and uncles. Why had I never thought of that? Just like I had never actually thought of a dead father until one morning in my early teens, exchanging confidences with a friend who had slept over at our house. There, lying on what we called the studio couch — a backless, pillowed couch that pulled out into a double bed — in the panelled den, I realized with a jolt: he died. He was twenty-five years old. Saying his age nearly took my breath away. He was a person, a young man with a life, in love, with worries and hopes and dreams. And he died, knowing perhaps as he bled internally that his life was ending. At twenty-five, in my mother's arms. Finally I felt the weight of the tragedy that had befallen my poor parents.

He remained a mystery all my life. My mother remarried eleven years later, soon after we came to Canada, and rarely spoke of him except his physical self. I had his mouth, she told me, my brother had his hazel eyes. But when I was older she would always call on April 29 to tell me, "Today was your father's birthday." I understand now that she really couldn't speak of him; she had never recovered from the shock of that nightmare, that terrible transition from one life as a young mother, in love with her beautiful young husband, to another life, born in a bloody night, where she was not just alone but blindingly lonely, a widow with two babies and no future, trying to get through each day.

Gold jewelry was a prized gift when I was growing up. Each girl child wore a gold bangle, and I inherited among my mother's jewelry some filigreed bracelets, including one with nuggets of gold and an inscription "To Gwen from Boze." But rather than these ornate bracelets and necklaces, my most treasured possession is a note she placed inside a small green jewelry box. Written in dark blue ink in my father's fine hand, the note is dated May 7, 1949, her birthday and six months before my birth: "To my own dear sweetheart. All my love for a happy birthday. Your first husband. That's me!"

Was this a private joke, or a sarcastic reference to his own mother's roster of husbands? Or did he sense that, as Aunt Gloria said, in his short life he would "have so little time for happiness"? My mother kept the plain white card in that simple box, secured with wide tape to preserve it, for the rest of her life.

And now, as I pore through these snapshots, seeing their lives played out in black and white, I'm aware of his happy times. Because his life ended there, at the age of twenty-five, these photographs are the only witness to where he started and what he became, the little French-speaking boy with the round face and curls who turned into the handsome, slender young man. There's one photo that stops me every time, on his identity papers, typewritten pages with a small headshot in the top left corner. I've made it bigger and bigger and bigger, every detail telling a story: those clear hazel eyes looking straight at the camera, the brows meeting in the middle — something I inherited, to my chagrin as I grew older — the wavy hair, the strong jaw and pointed chin, the straight nose, the thin upper lip, thick lower lip, the young, young face. All gone.

I knew that he died because he wouldn't see a doctor about the ulcer and refused even to go to the hospital on that fateful night. Why, the adult me thought, did she not insist? Why did she not call an ambulance? I would explain it to myself by imagining the deficiencies in Trinidad's medical system in the 1940s. But that's not the answer. I think the experience was just so sudden, so incomprehensible, and the outcome so unimaginable that she stayed with it, with him. She told me once, when she was much older and in the early stage of dementia, that for many, many nights after my father's death, "I used to dream of blood."

chapter 6

the nebenzahl tragedy

For centuries, motivated by exploration, adventure, commerce, poverty and, most recently, pleasure, we human beings have traversed the globe. Sadly, much of the emigration that so changed lives and the character of countries has been based on the exploitation of people and resources. Such was the case with my mother's ancestors, Madeiran peasants who left behind an unyielding land, crossing the ocean in sailing ships in the 1800s so they could labour in fields owned by their colonial landlords. All were desperate, hoping their new country would provide a stepping stone to the shores of a better life.

The family of my father, George Nebenzahl, also crossed the ocean in the nineteenth century, travelling from Europe and Britain to South America. His maternal grandparents, Edward Hart and Fanny Mordle, were of British origin, and had spent their lives in Georgetown. But the dearth of information on his mother's side was easily matched by the lack of details about his father's family. The few clues were so mysterious, so far removed from the childhood I knew, that for years the Nebenzahl story remained a blank space in my already fractured family history.

What I finally discovered about Joseph Nebenzahl, my grandfather, was that some of those puzzle pieces will never be found, and that the real story is a small episode in one of the world's most horrifying events.

Apart from the photograph placing him in Georgetown, I had no evidence of Joseph Nebenzahl except for a few documents in which he is named as my father's father, born in Belgium, possibly Antwerp. Over time I created for myself, from the little I heard, a scenario in which Joseph comes to South America and meets my grandmother there: he a salesman of some sort, plying his trade in the thriving colonies; she in her late adolescence, bored and beautiful, searching for a way out. I couldn't find records to support the other story that I was told, the one in which she goes off to Europe, meets him and then returns alone with my father George, pregnant with Gloria, leaving Joseph behind.

The more credible story is that a young Frances Ena Hart, who was born and grew up in Georgetown, met Joseph Nebenzahl there and decided to leave with him. She was sixteen years old, he was twenty-six. Joseph was French-speaking and somehow they ended up in Monte Carlo, where at the age of eighteen she gave birth to my father. Why there? Did she speak French? Were they married? There is a birth certificate, although on the original form my father's last name is given as Hart, not Nebenzahl.

But there are those photos, superficial evidence that my father was a happy child, doted on, cared for. And since Aunt Gloria was born in British Guiana and there is the one photograph of Joseph Nebenzahl taken in Georgetown, it looks like my grandparents returned to British Guiana and lived there, at least until my father was eight years old. Then what happened?

Throughout my childhood Aunt Gloria, my father's sister, would send Christmas cards from Pennsylvania, where she lived with her husband and young sons. There are a few snapshots of her in my father's album in what looks to be her late teens, standing against the wall of a house or by the roadside in a simple cotton dress, in the company of her mother and young half-sister. I have no photos of her interacting with my father, or with hers.

Then, when I was in my late twenties and starting my newspaper career, someone knocked at the door of a friend I was staying with in Ottawa. Gloria had appeared at my Montreal apartment looking for me, and my not-yet-husband told her where I was. She arrived unannounced on a summer afternoon, a pretty, dark-haired woman in the company of her husband Hank, solid and friendly, her quiet protector on this unusual errand. She introduced herself in a soft West Indian accent, still looking like the young woman in the family album. I was surprised — happy to see her but perplexed.

We took a walk along the Rideau Canal, and Gloria told me the reason for her visit: she had come to bring me some family jewelry she had inherited from her mother, my grandmother. "I have no daughters," she said, "so these belong to you." She opened a small jewelry box to show me a pair of pearl studs and a delicate diamond necklace. "They're yours," she said. The gift came from a past that I had barely acknowledged. I was grateful, but still was not ready to try to understand that story.

We kept in touch over the years, intermittently from my end but very methodically on hers — annual Christmas cards as well as postcards from Norway and other places she and Hank lived as he travelled for his work as an engineer. Then, when my daughter was nearly two years old, I took her with me to visit Gloria at her home on the edge of a Pennsylvania town full of handsome houses aproned by wide green lawns. I had wanted Gloria to connect with me, her brother's child, and with the granddaughter he never knew.

Truth is, I had lost my ambivalence about my paternal history. Now that I had a child, I was looking for traces of Gloria in her. I also wanted my aunt to describe to me the type of man my father was, and to recount any memories of her own mother and father. We stayed for a few days, and one afternoon sat down in her living room, filled with fine Quaker antiques, to talk about the past. But as soon as I began to ask questions, I realized that the act of remembering was too much for her. Gloria became choked up and agitated.

Her childhood was terrible, she told me. Her mother betrayed her. And she knew nothing about her father, Joseph. More than forty years later, she was still hurt and angry.

A few years passed, and I raised the subject again on the phone. Maybe because we weren't face to face, she began to speak about her mother, Ena Hart. She was one of three sisters, Gloria told me (one of them was named Evelyn, like the woman in the photograph), children of an English and Scottish couple. She had little to say about her grandparents, and I was treading so carefully that I didn't want to ask for more. She did describe her grandfather as a skinny guy, kind of mean, who worked for the waterworks. Her grandmother, she recalled, was very gentle.

And in her halting recollection of Joseph Nebenzahl, I found the man of my daydreams: a merchant, maybe a travelling salesman, who came to British Guiana from Europe. He returned in July 1923 aboard a Royal Dutch West India Mail Line ship sailing from Curaçao to Plymouth. Sixteen-year-old Ena went with him, registered as his wife. She gave birth to my father two years later in Monte Carlo. Based on the photos from Monte Carlo and Paris in my father's album, he was about four when Ena and Joseph came back to Georgetown with him. Ena gave birth to Gloria in British Guiana in 1929, and both mother and father were listed on her birth record. But Gloria would only speak of her mother. "Then she left the two of us with our grandparents," Gloria told me, "and she went back to Europe."

This didn't happen right away. That one photograph of the two couples shows that Joseph was there, at the house where my eight-year-old father was photographed, in 1933. Did Ena and Joseph leave together, a few years later? What were they going to do in Europe, pummelled by the Great Depression, with Adolf Hitler now the chancellor of Germany? And what about their children?

Maybe they were planning to send for George and Gloria later. But in the ensuing few years, Ena left one husband and then another and might not have returned even then, although Europe was at war. The catalyst was the death of her mother in British Guiana, leaving no one to care for the children. Little Gloria could hardly wait, imagining the happiness of their reunion, the wonder of having a mother by her side. Ena, however, returned with a child in her arms, fathered by another husband, Serge Abagoff. "I thought she was finally coming back to be my mother," Gloria said bitterly, "but she only wanted a babysitter."

Her mother, she told me, moved in with their grandfather and went out at night. "I wanted to get to know her, but it was very hard," she said. "She only wanted to have fun." Gloria loved and cared for her half-sister Nina, but she never found that maternal figure for whom she had longed. Quite the opposite. Her mother married again, a man named Jack Spratt, another bad match. Ena's relationships frequently failed, Gloria recalled. "It's like she didn't grow up, and after a while the men she was involved with saw it."

For Gloria, even escaping into an early marriage didn't help. Her mother had married yet again, this time a Portuguese man, and Gloria attached herself to his brother, marrying him while still a teenager and giving birth to a son. But he was abusive, she said, and finally she fled to Trinidad with her child, helped by friends she made while working at Grandfather's store. My father, who was living in Trinidad at the time of Gloria's flight out of British Guiana, also helped his sister to run away.

Gloria found a solid, comfortable life. She married Hank, an American soldier, an engineer she met in Trinidad, and he remained devoted to her for the next sixty or more years. Yet the trauma of her upbringing, the great sadness and bitterness of her childhood, continued to haunt her. The only way she could deal with it, I realized, was never to talk about it, and she steadfastly refused to travel back in time to recall her own father, whether he was with her growing up, what kind of man he was. These traumatic memories still had power over her, and for the rest of her life she could not face contemplating them.

I daydreamed a story for Ena, like I did for my father and grandfather. Born in 1907 in Georgetown, she was the daughter of hardscrabble British working-class parents, and the family lived on the edge of poverty, emotional as well as physical. I imagine that as she grew, she chafed at being dominated by a mean-spirited father, despite the kindness of her mother. Did she set out to parlay her beauty into escape? Did she believe she was destined for better things? By the time she was in her teens, it was the early 1920s. In the photos she is striking, with clear hazel eyes, a heart-shaped face, a lithe body. I could see her pining away in that quiet tropical city, longing for adventure.

In my imagination, the feelings of being stifled only increased as Ena grew. So when she met the travelling salesman from Belgium, who spoke French and promised her the glamour of life in Europe, she left without hesitation. She was just sixteen, very young to be embarking on such a major voyage, but I imagined that her chance of an adventurous life mattered more than any parental disapproval. Or maybe they didn't care. Since France was engaged in postwar rebuilding and workers were flooding into the country, Joseph's chances of finding work would have been good. The Riviera in the 1920s was glittering and free-spirited. Young women cut their hair into bobs or marcelled waves and smoked cigarettes with long holders; the privileged drove sports cars and danced all night.

In my story, Joseph with his slicked-back hair and easy smile was a croupier in the casino in Monaco, and maybe counted among his patrons the likes of Ernest Hemingway and F. Scott Fitzgerald, Cole Porter and Coco Chanel. Described in various official documents as a "merchant," he travelled by his wits, and the young couple took advantage of the boisterous party town of Monte Carlo, even if they didn't have much money. It was a sun-drenched life, lived mainly in cafes, so it didn't much matter that their home was in the poorer part of town.

Both were stylish, and I can imagine that even with little they were so good-looking that they could hide a frayed collar or thin soles. I don't know if Ena had any intellectual pursuits or any wishes other than pleasure. Getting pregnant must have put a damper on their plans for a carefree life, although my father looks well-loved in those early photos. And she must have managed to learn French to live there; they gave their baby the name Georges Louis Paul and my father spoke only French when he arrived in Georgetown as a small child.

But that strange pride I felt in her, a beautiful woman who didn't play by the rules — the photo of her with that short, boyish haircut and one-piece bathing suit was the backdrop to my fantasy — dissipated when I learned of the pain of Aunt Gloria's childhood. My grandmother's five (or four) husbands included not only Joseph Nebenzahl but also the supposed White Russian count Serge Abagoff, the father of her third child, Nina, and the Portuguese man who surely embodied all that was wrong with her emotional intelligence. This man was the brother of the abusive husband Auntie Gloria had run away from in Georgetown. The fact that Ena and her own daughter were married to two brothers has a seedy ring, even today.

Eventually Ena added a final partner or husband; in the photo album my father tags him as "Bill." And then, in her early forties, when my parents were living in Trinidad before their wedding, she died suddenly of an aneurysm. Whatever he felt, however much her self-centredness hurt him, my father's response was to retreat. He so disapproved of her, my mother told me years later, that "when she died, he didn't even go to her funeral."

◇

And where did my grandfather go? I had been told as a child that Nebenzahl was a Belgian name, and from time to time a German-speaking person would comment on its strange meaning, translating it as "the nearby number" or "the figure next door." Then, sometime in the 1980s, a letter arrived in the newsroom of the Montreal newspaper where I worked from a David Nebenzahl from California, wondering if I was related somehow and citing ancestors with names like Moishe and Abraham. When my first child was born, a Montreal man phoned, saying his last name was Nebenzahl and he came from a Jewish family in Poland. Paul Nebenzahl from Chicago contacted me, convinced I was a long-lost Jewish cousin. I was confused. "No, no," I told them all. "I'm not Jewish. I grew up in South America. I'm Portuguese Catholic, from Madeira. I don't know about the rest."

And anyway, I thought, Judaism is matrilineal.

But it kept bothering me, a little voice murmuring in my head: "Who cares if it's matrilineal, that's just a religious doctrine ..." I was so thoroughly disconnected from Judaism — I come from the tropics, from warmth and colour. I know the Latin mass! To me, Jewish tradition seemed gloomy: men in dark clothing from Eastern Europe, whose culture I didn't understand at all.

Yet I continued to wonder. Was my grandfather Jewish? And if so, what had happened to him when he returned to Europe? My grandparents had gone back to France sometime after 1933, and there's no evidence that Joseph ever returned to South America. Ena had taken that mysterious trip to New York in 1934, and despite giving an address in Paris as her home, it looks like she never returned to Europe. She was in New York when she met Serge Abagoff and called it quits on her first marriage.

Sometime around 1938, the second marriage was also over and Ena had returned with a new baby to her pining nine-year-old daughter and teenage son. Without doubt, if Joseph was now in Paris, he was in the centre of a gathering storm. The Munich agreement of September 30, 1938, signed by France, Germany, Britain and Italy, paved the way for Hitler's army to march into the Sudetenland. A year later, in response to Hitler's invasion of Poland, Britain and France declared war on Germany.

Poland was quickly defeated, and then German forces invaded Norway and Denmark. They began their assault on western Europe in May 1940, and on June 22, France signed an agreement with Germany, providing for the German occupation of the northern half of the country and the establishment of the collaborationist Vichy regime in the south. The Germans occupied Paris, and while the city was physically spared, its citizens were coerced, humiliated and in many cases killed by the Nazis.

For years after those calls about my ancestry, I would occasionally search up the name Joseph Nebenzahl, never expecting to find any connection. I tried linking the name to Poland, Belgium, France, Monaco — all yielded nothing. And then I made a startling discovery. The website of the Shoah Memorial in Paris lists French citizens killed by the Nazis in the Second World War. On that list was the name Joseph Nebenzahl. According to the Shoah website, this Joseph Nebenzahl had been born in 1895 or 1896, right around the time of my grandfather's birth. He was a merchant. He lived in Paris.

It was a terrible place to be. No sooner was the city under Nazi rule than the accustomed life of the Jewish population was destroyed. The Nazis barred Jews from working as lawyers and doctors, and they were forbidden from entering restaurants and other public places. Their property was seized. By May 1942, following Adolf Eichmann's directive, the deportation of French Jews to Auschwitz began and they were required to self-identify by wearing the yellow Star of David badge.

This was difficult terrain for me to navigate. After years of lacklustre searching, I now had a result I couldn't ignore. Maybe it was journalistic curiosity, but more likely a certain inevitability I was beginning to feel about my story, that made me keep searching. Through a friend who volunteered at the Holocaust Museum in Montreal, I was given the name Jackie Schwartz, a researcher who lived in Belgium. We started to chat by email, and soon Jackie was asking me the questions I should have asked myself years ago.

Is this my grandfather, whose name appears on a monument to the Jews of France who died in Nazi concentration camps? Jackie seemed to think it was possible. This Joseph Nebenzahl was indeed born in Belgium, Antwerp to be exact, but his family were Polish Jews from the region of Galicia. She discovered the identity of Joseph Nebenzahl's parents: his father, Psachje Paul Nebenzahl, born in 1865 in Poland, had married Judes Schulsinger in 1892 in Krakow. They had two children: Necha Natalia Nebenzahl, born in 1893 in Krakow, and Joseph Nebenzahl, born on December 31, 1896, in Antwerp. Evidently the Nebenzahls had emigrated to Belgium — in 1920 Joseph was serving in the Belgian Army — and by 1928 the family had become naturalized citizens.

This discrepancy of birth years, 1895 in some documents, 1896 in others, is not unusual, Jackie told me. And there were other clues pointing to this being my grandfather. First, he gave his son, my father, the middle name Paul — his own father's middle name. And the central database in the World Holocaust Remembrance Centre, Yad Vashem, lists Joseph Nebenzahl's birth on the same day and month as my grandfather's, December 31.

To these clues, I have added a piece of research that solidifies my connection with this man. Continuing to tell myself that my ancestry centred on Madeira and South America, I had shelved results from the DNA test that I took a decade ago when I joined the Ancestry website. I realized, finally, that the result constitutes clear proof. On my mother's side, I am almost entirely Portuguese. No surprise there. But on my father's side, the DNA results show that I am at least twenty-five per cent Jewish, from Poland and Moldova — the lands from which Joseph Nebenzahl's family emerged.

◇

Ena had travelled from France to New York City in 1934, giving an address in Paris. Is this where Joseph continued to live? By the end of 1940, according to Yad Vashem, the Jews of France had been "denuded of their civil rights and their property, dismissed from the civil service, and expelled from their businesses. Tens of thousands of businesses and thousands of apartments were confiscated from Jews." To make things worse for Joseph, victims of anti-Jewish policy at this time were mainly foreign Jews, rather than those who held French citizenship. Joseph Nebenzahl, with his Belgian citizenship, would have been considered a foreign Jew.

He must have been, like so many others, caught up in the frantic need to survive. Was he victimized, living in hiding, without enough money to plan an escape? Where could he go? By October 1941, European Jews were banned from emigrating. The situation was dire in Paris, where half the Jewish population, some 43,000 people, had been sent to concentration camps by the time the war ended, and 34,000 had died there. But records show that Joseph was picked up in Marseille, not Paris. At some point, he must have gone to the port city in hopes of escaping.

Thousands of Jews had travelled to Marseille because it was considered a sanctuary city, the only large port in the so-called Free Zone open to the rest of the world, and an embarkation point for those trying to flee Europe. Many important Jewish intellectuals and artists, including Marc Chagall and Hannah Arendt, hid out in Marseille before their escape to North America.

In the summer of 1940, Nazi control over southern France tightened. Hitler declared Marseille full of subversives, calling it the "asylum for the international underworld." After the Allied invasion of North Africa in 1942, Vichy France blocked the exit from the city to stop Resistance fighters from joining the Allies. As historian Marianne Enckell described the situation: "France was a trap in a bigger European trap closing up. And Marseille was a rat trap."

Then, in January 1943, with the Nazis in control, French police carried out mass arrests of Marseille residents, and in the following month an entire neighbourhood in the Old Port was razed. More and more Jewish families and refugees were rounded up and deported. It struck me as I read the literature that this word "deport," which in its best sense means to carry oneself with dignity and in its worst means to be sent back to your home country, had neither of these meanings here. In this context, "deport" meant death.

I imagine Joseph Nebenzahl alone, quite destitute at this point, making his way to Marseille maybe in 1940, with the largest influx of refugees. Then in May 1944, not three months before France was liberated, he was caught up in a wave of arrests, perhaps on one of the trains leaving or arriving in the city. He was sent to Drancy, in the northeast of Paris, an internment camp run by the Nazis and guarded by French gendarmes that had, by that time, become a concentration camp. Located near three train stations, this was the stopping place before the final deportation. Joseph arrived in Drancy from Marseille on May 19, 1944, a Shoah Memorial researcher told Jackie, and was given internment number 22247. Then she offered what I considered the final clue that he was indeed my father's father: "His middle name was Georges."

By May 30, he was on another train, identified not as a merchant but as a cook. Here is a deportation document from the Shoah Memorial in Paris, which was sent to Jackie:

27

626	MOISE Rémy	22.I2.99	Ingenieur	234I5
627	MOISE Simone	22. I.44	Ohne	234I7
628	MOISE Suzanne	7. 3.05	Ohne	234I6
629	MOLINE Serge	22. 8.24	Arbeiter	23408
630	MONTEL Andrée	7.I2.97	Verkauferin	23359
63I	MONTEL Edmée	27. 3.02	Verkauferin	23360
632	MONTEL Fanny	I0. 4.75	Angestellte	23358
633	MORDO Michel	I5. 6.9I	Verkaufer	22232
634	MOSES Betty	I9.II.89	Ohne	22493
635	NADEL Isaac	I9.II.80	Elektriker	23250
636	NAKACHE Frida	24.I0.77	Ohne	2257I
637	NAKACHE Simone	I7. I.67	Kaufmann	22570
638	NATANSON Hedwige	22. 9.28	Studentin	22087
639	NATANSON Stephanie	5.5.98	Lehrerin	22086
640	NATANSON Wladislas	30.6.98	Elektriker	22085
64I	NAVARRO Semtov	I4.I0.84	Buchhalter	22494
642	NAVARRO Lucia	I4. 7.00	Ohne	22495
643	NAVARRO Maurice	I6. 2.27	Student	22496
644	NEBENZAHL Joseph	31.I2.95	Koch	22247
645	NEGRI Yechoua	I5. 3.03	Kaufmann	I8755
646	NEUKIRCHER Curt	29.II.84	Schauspieler	22472
647	NEUKIRCHER Erna	I3. I.86	Ohne	22473
648	NUGELBLATT Dora	6. 3.03	Frisörin	22952
649	NUSSBAUM Erika	28.II.09	Ohne	2I274
650	OBERDORFER Clara	5. I.70	Ohne	23086

```
Prénom, nom: Joseph NEBENZAHL
Date de naissance: 31/12/1895
Année de naissance: 1895
Profession: Cuisinier
Numéro de convoi: N°75
Date de départ du convoi: 30/05/1944
Lieu de départ du convoi: Drancy
Camp de destination: Auschwitz
Matricule d'internement: 22247
```

Transport 75 from the train station at Drancy left France for the Auschwitz-Birkenau extermination camp in Poland on May 30, 1944. This was one of twenty deportations carried out over a period of thirteen months, expelling approximately 20,000 Jews from France, both native and foreign nationals. The transports were overseen by Alois Brunner, Eichmann's assistant, who had already directed the deportation of Jews from Austria, Berlin and Greece. In July 1943 he became chief of the "special unit" for Jewish Affairs in France.

The Nazis' fastidious record-keeping was collapsing by May 1944, and three months later, Allied troops reached Paris. In mid-January 1945, as the Soviet Army approached, the SS began evacuating Auschwitz, forcing more than 60,000 prisoners to walk westward in the bitter cold, in what came to be known as death marches. Thousands had been hastily killed in the camps in the days before these marches began. As the United States Holocaust Memorial Museum states, "SS guards shot anyone who fell behind or could not continue … Possibly as many as 15,000 prisoners died during the evacuation marches from Auschwitz and the subcamps."

I was unable to find a death certificate, which is not unusual, says Jackie. But I have a copy of a deportation document in which a man named Joseph Nebenzahl, born on 31/12/1895, domiciled in Paris, was sent to Drancy on Transport 75. In one corner of the document is a small phrase: n'a pas survécu. Did not survive.

So why Monte Carlo? My daydream about Joseph working at the casino might have been true, but Jackie observed a strange anomaly on a document that I had owned for years. On the birth certificate in my possession, my father's name is written as Hart, Georges Louis Paul, and his mother is named Frances Ena Hart. He is given her last name and although the father's name is filled in lower down in the document as Joseph Nebenzahl, it is written in another hand. It looks like an afterthought.

Jackie managed to acquire a copy of a second official document, the Bulletin de Naissance, issued by the Mairie de Monaco. Again, it gives my father's name as Georges Louis Paul Hart, not Nebenzahl. His mother is Francis Ena Hart, aged twenty-eight, "without profession." The truth is, she was born in 1907; in 1925 she was eighteen, not twenty-eight. So the story I heard in my childhood — that she went off to Europe when she was just sixteen years old — is very likely true. There are a few other names on the document, surprising names: the "declaration of the infant" was witnessed by Luigi Curti, industrialist, age thirty-four, a native of Turin. The document was made in the presence, and with the signatures, of Jacques Raymond, age twenty-eight, without profession, and Georges Rolfo, thirty-one, a hotelier, both domiciled in Monaco. Were they friends, acquaintances, lovers or just a couple of guys at the Mairie who were needed as additional signatories? And what relationship did this eighteen-year-old woman have to Luigi Curti?

Most important, the part of the document reserved for the other parent's name is entirely crossed out. Why is Joseph Nebenzahl's name not there at all? My heart sinks when I see this. It could be, I tell myself, that in this time of rife anti-Semitism, Ena Hart was trying to protect her baby by giving him a non-Jewish surname. Or maybe it's another example of my grandmother not living her life by the conventional rules and giving birth without being married.

Where was Joseph when my father was born? Were he and Ena estranged at that point, only to reconcile later? Is that why he's not on one birth certificate and named in a manner that looks like an afterthought in another? But they brought little George with them back to South America, where Gloria was born in 1929. And his name is clearly on her birth certificate. But a marriage certificate between Ena and Joseph has never materialized. Did they never marry? Is it possible he isn't my grandfather at all?

I had learned much more than I thought possible about Joseph Nebenzahl, although the unknown bits have taken on an even more mysterious cast. I see him as a happy-go-lucky type, dark hair swept back from a wide forehead, hooded eyes, maybe the kind of man always seeking an elusive fortune. I know that he spent at least a decade with Ena, and in that time was a father to two little children. Then something convinced the couple to return to Europe, abandoning their children to caretakers. What was so important that they abdicated the responsibility of parenthood?

Things fell apart soon after. Ena left him in Paris. Did Joseph think about pursuing her, or returning to South America to be with his family? Finally, reading the chilling evidence of my grandfather's internment, I imagine a haunted, desperate man, alone, bereft. During the terror of the roundup, the transport to Drancy, to Auschwitz, did he think about the children he had left behind?

I have struggled with the task of transforming this invisible man with an unknown history into a living character. His choices led to misfortune, yes, but ultimately led to my brother and me. So I have decided to claim you, Joseph Nebenzahl, as my grandfather. I do this in full knowledge of Jackie's uncertainty, at the same time knowing that her research has never revealed another Joseph Nebenzahl with any connection to this story. The names have convinced me: naming your child Georges Louis Paul when your middle name is Georges and your father's name is Paul is just too much of a coincidence.

My poor father. Like any child, he must have been hoping for his father's return, and I wonder at what point he realized that he would never see him again. A missing father — whose fate was never mentioned, likely never revealed — and a mother who was there physically but not dependable. No wonder he grew up edgy and careful. Is that why he was so drawn to this young Portuguese woman? My mother's strength of character and the absolute certainty of her family's loyalty and support must have been breathtaking to him.

chapter 7

a new world

My brother and I first travelled to Canada with our grandparents in 1956. We came by ship, staying for a few months with our mother and Auntie Thelma, all crowded into their small apartment on Queen Mary Road in Montreal. I had always thought that the grownups simply believed we needed to visit our mother, but later I realized that it might have been a trial run, to see how we would cope. Then the four of us went back home. In 1959, after our second voyage to this cold, welcoming place, George and I never returned to British Guiana.

Were we worried about what awaited us? My brother and I never talked about what our lives would be like at the end of the trip. Like most children, we were immersed in what was happening around us, and a sea voyage was pure adventure. Each time, we travelled more than three thousand nautical miles, first in the Caribbean Sea and then the Atlantic, skirting the coasts of Mexico and the United States.

For nearly two weeks the great, wide ocean was guaranteed all our attention. We were thrilled to be leaving land behind, waking up to wavelets glittering in the sunlight or a sea as calm as glass right to the horizon or, best of all, a soup of stormy whitecaps below darkening skies. Though we felt like there was only water everywhere, travelling by ship from South America meant that we passed by or visited some of the prettiest islands in the Caribbean.

Since no passenger ships left from Georgetown in those days, we travelled on one of the many freighters belonging to Saguenay Terminals of Montreal. These ships had a job to do, stopping en route to pick up or deliver freight on behalf of the Aluminum Company of Canada. On one trip, I remember the ship being loaded with bauxite at the port in Trinidad. I stood at the rails in the late afternoon watching huge machines scoop and dump, depositing the pale dust in the hold of the ship, the only time I ever viewed the island country where I was born. As I gazed from the deck at the verdant coastline and the darkening hills, I felt a tug in my heart, a longing to somehow rewind the picture, imagining my infant self in a house on that island, in the arms of her loving parents.

For me, the most exciting part of travelling by ship was when that dot on the horizon transformed into an island rising from the sea and then to a living place with small boats milling around our large one, people calling out, the buildings of the town looming larger as our big ship slowly manoeuvred its way to the dock. I never knew why we made so many stops; Trinidad was just one of the islands on our route to and from Canada. We docked in Jamaica, St. Lucia, Guadeloupe and Antigua and spent a wonderful day wandering about the dazzlingly colourful city of Santo Domingo in the Dominican Republic, where street vendors sold multicoloured clothing and sweet drinks.

On our return sailing after the first trip to Canada, we stayed for a few days in Barbados. I was fascinated by the pale sand beach and sparkling turquoise water, just a stone's throw from the back door of the guest house owned by my Uncle Frank, the second oldest of my six uncles, and his Dutch Indian wife Edna. In Georgetown, we lived on the coast, but all we saw was a seawall and what seemed like miles of dry mud. I loved wandering through this garden where only beach grasses and a few tropical flowers grew in the thin soil, enclosed by a picket fence with a gate that opened to an expanse of tawny gold sand as far as the eye could see. At the dining table inside the simple wooden house, filmy curtains lifting in the ocean breezes, we enjoyed delicious food made by Auntie Edna, who stood by the stove in a colourful cotton shift, her long reddish-brown hair tied back in a thick braid.

Then there was life on board ship. The crews, neither Canadian nor British, came from a noticeably different culture, which meant I rarely understood what they were saying. The food we ate was new to me, sometimes not great but always different, which I loved. I remember little bottles of soft drinks, fizzy orange and lemon. Because there was room for only a few passengers on these ships, we were regularly invited to sit at the captain's table. I could tell from Granny's expression and polite tone that we were very honoured and needed to be well-behaved.

And we were surrounded by sailors, young men who were there to run the ship, although I'm pretty sure that a couple of children were a novelty to them, especially my dark-haired little brother with his boyish curiosity about moving parts and engines. One friendly sailor even gave George a miniature outboard motor. His fascination with it was a real worry for me because I was his self-appointed guardian, and all this attention made it hard going.

Granny had told us that, once we left our home in B.G., life would be much riskier for young children. They were kidnapped sometimes, she said, taken away and never seen again, because people in other countries did bad things. She might have been trying to keep us alert, but I was constantly terrified that my brother would disappear on board ship. Imagine my panic one afternoon when I couldn't find him. Only after searching frantically did I come upon him in that sailor's cabin, running the motor in the sink. Easy-going as ever, George came along when I shooed him out of there. The friendly sailors were no match for my ferocious caretaking.

I can't recall ever getting seasick or feeling anxious about the weather as we sailed along the Atlantic coast. Stormy days were the most exciting if you weren't afraid, which we never were. Sometimes it heaved enough that your tummy felt the churn, but most of the time we were up and about, especially during the return voyage from Canada to South America because we were transporting cattle. George and I regularly visited the dozen or so cows, eyeing them from a respectful distance in their large wooden pens. They didn't feel the way we did about storms; the terrified animals bellowed, eyes rolling, as the ship lurched.

On our final trip, in the late fall, entering Canadian waters felt like a message: a momentous landscape, pristine but cold, beautiful but a little forbidding. I could feel a change in the atmosphere, a sense of an ending to the voyage as the ship sailed into the mouth of the St. Lawrence River, slowing to prepare for the boarding of the river pilot. Then we moved toward the Saguenay en route to Port Alfred, where we were to unload the bauxite. I never spotted the harbour seals or whales that congregate where the Saguenay and St. Lawrence meet and fresh river water flows into the cold salt water. We were too busy looking up, awestruck, at the majestic surroundings.

The soaring rock walls of that fjord, a deep gash in the Precambrian rock gouged by glaciers of the last ice age, with cliffs rising to 350 metres above the water, gave Granny an opportunity to honour her God. As we passed the nine-metre-high statue of the Virgin Mary in white and blue, pinned against the rocks in 1881 at the mouth of Baie Trinité, we stood on the deck in the chill air, making the sign of the cross. Notre Dame du Saguenay looked surreal, oddly moving as she gazed down upon us, her hands closed in prayer to bless all passing travellers. The ship's bells rang out, reverberating against the rocky walls.

We were innocents, George and I, not at all attuned to the displacement that we were undergoing. We never asked ourselves how we would feel about life in a new country, about giving up our tropical childhoods. Without realizing it, we were the subjects Michael Ondaatje described in the 2012 essay "Mongrel Art," who "arrived carrying a past vision and history but also that necessary half-open door in themselves so they can discover the new land." The first ocean voyage was an adventure, but I can't say that I ever told myself, once we were in Canada: "I choose this place; this is where my brother and I are going to live."

For my mother and grandparents, that first trip must have made it clear that a mother who headed off to secretarial work each day was not going to be able to handle having two young children. Auntie Thelma got married soon after and moved out, so how could my mother manage on her own? Daycare, single parenthood: these were not easy routes in the 1950s.

She lived with her sister Thelma, who was also a secretary, so most of our days during that first visit in the summer of 1956 were spent with our grandparents in the apartment on Queen Mary Road in Montreal. Four- and five-storey apartment buildings, most in red brick, some trimmed with faux timber beams, lined the busy thoroughfare. There were shops up and down the road and the feeling of a big sky, since the street was not far from the treed expanse of Mount Royal.

But for Granny, this area was special because it was crowned by one of her favourite places, St. Joseph's Oratory. Founded by Brother André, a caretaker and humble lay brother, this was the holiest site in the city of Montreal, and my grandmother revered it. Hundreds of crutches lined the walls inside the church, relics of the miracles supposedly wrought by Brother André. Entry was managed on foot by climbing the masses of stone steps, nearly three hundred leading up to the basilica. The real test, though, was the ninety-nine wooden steps for those who felt compelled to make the climb on their knees. I don't know whether Granny ever did that — I'm betting she didn't — but everyone knew that she considered this to be the rite of a true pilgrim. The basilica, with its massive, oversize dome topped with a cross that was lit every night, created an optical illusion of incredible height, given its location on high ground. It was impressive, a far cry from the original church on the site, Brother André's little shrine, which measured only five by six metres.

We spent the weekends visiting family and sometimes taking excursions to other holy sites like the Basilica of Sainte-Anne-de-Beaupré, so Granny could once again worship at a shrine. Sometimes one of the siblings would visit. On one memorable occasion Uncle Steve arrived from Nova Scotia, where he worked on Coast Guard icebreakers. He was a jokester, full of fun, which might have been why he didn't realize what I knew, that afternoon he took us for a walk down Queen Mary Road: the streets of Montreal were full of kidnappers. When he left us outside the smoke shop near the apartment so he could buy cigarettes, I promptly seized my brother's hand and took off back to the apartment. I was severely reprimanded for disobeying Uncle — I had no idea how he must have felt when he came outside and realized we were gone — but there was no way I was going to leave my little brother standing on the sidewalk, a sitting duck for a wily Canadian abductor.

We were used to lots of space for playing, outside in the sunshine or in our grandparents' large home. Was that why George and I spent so much time jumping on the furniture and bounding around the living room? Much later I was told that our noisy behaviour during that first visit led to the sisters deciding (or being asked) to leave the apartment. They chose a significantly bigger place, but the reason for this was not evident to me until we arrived in Canada that second time: my mother had met someone.

Granny and Grandfather didn't sit down and talk to us about the move in the autumn of 1959, but in the midst of our playtime and school days, George and I must have registered some added activity. When the day of our departure arrived, I don't recall expressing any emotion about it, but my body gave way. We were to board the ship in late afternoon, and by lunchtime my head began to pound. It was a headache, the first of my life, previewing an adolescence filled with debilitating attacks. I recall viewing the world horizontally, lying on the bottom bunk in the boys' room, feeling relief only when Granny gently rubbed Vicks VapoRub on my forehead and temples, the burning sensation dulling the pain. I see now that it was my heart that ached in helpless sorrow.

Cookie was the first to bring a gift. "For you, Miss Donna," she said shyly, handing me a handmade cloth laundry bag on a little wooden hanger. On the front, the figure of a bunny rabbit wearing a red-and-white striped shirt and suspenders. "Rub-a-dub-in-the-tub Laundry" was stitched at the rabbit's feet. I have it still, more than sixty years later. How I wish that I could have held Cookie's rough hands, told her how much I was going to miss her. But my mind was just too full of pain because that throbbing headache wouldn't recede.

Then Auntie Elaine approached me as I lay on the bed, her blue eyes huge behind her glasses. I had spent my life playing with her daughters Ros and Janis, running in and out of her house, just behind ours. Was she imagining what it would be like without my brother and myself? Auntie handed me a small box. "To remember us by, child," she said. Inside, a treasured gift: a watch with pale leather straps, its white face sporting the cheery figure of Mickey Mouse.

Our arrival in Montreal was a blur, a waking dream barely brightened by the double-breasted coat in soft red wool that the dressmaker had made for me. After some weeks, my grandparents returned to Georgetown without us. I can't remember their leaving, can't recall saying goodbye or crying or feeling lonely, but there was an austerity to this new life that I had never imagined. Just like I never imagined Granny and Grandfather would not be the centrepieces of my everyday nor faced the reality that I would never return to my home on Brickdam Street.

But now, here in Canada, that sunny past just disappeared. Deeply, deeply, I felt that I was on an uncertain path, although I never consciously entertained any feelings of longing for my earlier life. George and I had entered a new country, a place described by memoirist Eva Hoffman in which the past appears suddenly on the other side of a great divide, held in our memory but no longer connected to the present.

I knew that we were here because this was a better life — although I had not known how insecure our future in South America had become. So at first I just plodded along, out of place, but accepting that this is where I was meant to be. Like Auntie Gloria before me, I could finally have a mother by my side, be the apple of her eye.

Auntie Thelma had married by this time, and my mother and Uncle Charlie now lived in an apartment in a 1950s warren of three-storey red-brick buildings with wrought-iron balconies that took up a square block in the west end of the city. They were peopled with hardworking families, some satisfied to stay there, others determined to move on, another wave of the many immigrants who made Montreal their home. This village of many ethnicities felt safe, easy; without anyone saying so, I understood that these were people just like us.

I was ten years old, and every morning my brother and I left the apartment for the twenty-minute trek to St. Ignatius of Loyola elementary school, along grey sidewalks, over the railroad tracks and, after another few blocks, up to a stately buff-brick building with a large asphalt playground surrounded by frost fencing. What a difference from being ferried by bicycle or van to the Ursuline convent, along sunny roads with grassy verges. The only sidewalks in Georgetown were on the main shopping streets.

I wore knee socks, it was late fall, and my knees were so cold they would sometimes get a bluish cast. My little red coat had been replaced by a ski jacket and I don't remember if I wore a hat or gloves. But I didn't mind the cold, not at all. It was so mysterious, this sensation of chill on the body, one that I had never experienced.

Just as mysterious in this strange country was the way these buildings were filled with apartments, dozens of them, each containing an entire house. I marvelled at that. The apartment, tucked away on the first floor of a building, number 7461, with only two apartments per floor, had three bedrooms, one for my Uncle Charlie, one for my mother, and one for my brother and myself. At the end of the long hallway near the bedrooms stood a tall space heater in dark brown metal, designed to warm the place during the cold winter months. The living room had windows on either side of a door leading to the small balcony.

Another door, from the kitchen, opened onto the back of the apartment with a shed on the landing and stairs leading to a parking lot shared by all the buildings.

The rooms were small, nothing like the airy spaces in my grandparents' home in Georgetown, but I didn't mind this little apartment. Perhaps it gave me a feeling of security, the comfort of knowing my way around easily. A shiny black front door opened onto a narrow hall where my mother had placed a telephone table, one of those joined table-and-seat concoctions. Here she would sit, chatting on the black phone with a rotary dial; we hadn't graduated to avocado or beige.

To the right of the doorway, my favourite room: the tiny, white-tiled bathroom where I encountered my first bathtub. What a novelty to lie in a bath, especially once I discovered that Ivory Soap floated. I began spending a lot of time bathing, partly to warm my chilled body but mostly to escape into my dream world. Because this was the point at which I began to choose daydreaming over reality. So simple, really, to forget the present — which I didn't think was so terrible, not at all, but things were so much better in my own world of stories. I had no cousins to play with, no games of make believe. Those maidens in distress could only be rescued in my imagination.

And I pored over books, any books. I even became attached to a bunch of songbooks owned by one of my aunts, containing the words to many popular songs. Soon I knew all the words to "Ivory Tower" by Cathy Carr and "The Wayward Wind" by

Gogi Grant, and some version of the tunes as well. I sang in the bath and sometimes for family, who surrounded us, even in this distant land. Uncle Charlie still shared the apartment and my Auntie Olga, who had left for Canada a few years earlier with Uncle Mike, lived upstairs in the same building with Uncle Mike and two small sons.

But Auntie Olga, so full of fun and activity when I knew her in South America, didn't seem happy here. Because my mother worked, we were effectively latchkey kids and would go to Auntie Olga's after school for a snack. On a few of those afternoons we found her in bed, her two little blue-eyed boys running amok in the apartment.

Still, Auntie Olga was always there for us. Soon she was called upon to take us for our polio vaccines, a foil against the terrifying viral illness paralytic poliomyelitis, a huge worry when we arrived in Canada. There were nearly nine thousand cases and five hundred deaths in 1953, the deadliest year of the epidemic, when the country was still without the vaccine. In 1959, the year we arrived, Canada experienced one of the highest incidence rates ever recorded in this country. In Quebec, where the majority of polio cases had occurred, the unvaccinated rate was seventy-seven per cent.

George and I knew nothing about the thousands of children who had been struck down and paralyzed by the virus, only that all children needed to be vaccinated. So, another first: a ride on a city bus. I recall a cloudy day, climbing on the snub-nosed brown and grey bus with Auntie Olga and my brother, then gazing about at the people getting on and off, not chatty or loud or laughing as they would have been in Georgetown. These folks were quiet, going about their business without a lot of eye contact.

Returning home, as we sat on the long benches that ran along the sides near the back of the bus, I felt my left arm aching where the needle had jabbed me. But polio meant nothing tangible to me until I became close friends in high school with a girl who had contracted polio and spent a year in hospital, emerging with one leg shorter than the other despite post-corrective surgery. How courageous she was, I thought, and how that lonely, painful year must have challenged her.

It was impossible to avoid another great perk of this working-class neighbourhood, besides being an easy walk to school and to St. Ignatius of Loyola church, where George and I attended mass every Sunday: our apartment was located just across the street from Elmhurst Dairy, Montreal's most popular ice cream shop, and a city landmark. On the exterior wall of the beige brick building with its Mediterranean-style curved roof tiles, two beautiful oversize cow heads loomed, looking both stately and kind. They were Elsie and Elmer, one a velvety brown Jersey cow, the other a black and white Holstein. Behind the brick façade, the stainless steel dairy processing plant was also a crowd magnet, especially on a hot summer weekend.

Sometimes the lineups snaked out of the building as Montrealers waited to try the many flavours that made this dairy an institution. The interior, a dazzling cavern of white subway tiles, had high counters on two sides and metal pipe fencing that herded customers into lines for service. The countermen wore white aprons and paper hats. It was here that I first tasted pistachio ice cream — green ice cream! — in a cone, so different from my grandmother's hand-churned vanilla. It felt good to eat that ice cream cone, sitting on the balcony of the apartment that looked out at those sweet-faced cows.

Winter, I discovered, was a season of snowmen and skating, but also of icy sidewalks and hidden threats. I became painfully aware of this one cold day as I approached the outer door of the apartment building with its diagonal metal safety bar and decided to stick out my tongue. Like many children before me, I learned that a warm tongue is no protection against an ice-cold piece of metal. I stood there, panicked, as my tongue stuck to the bar, and only by accidentally breathing heavily did I manage to loosen it without tearing the tender flesh. It was a season of darkness, too, so getting home right after school was critical. I hadn't forgotten Granny's lessons about big cities and bad people, and even though I felt safe on Upper Lachine Road, no way I was going to pass by the yawning cavern at the back of the buildings, where the back stairs converged on the parking areas, in the dark.

I started school in November, and since the school year had already begun, I had the discomfort of entering a group where children already knew each other. Besides, I was a knobby-kneed girl who wore glasses and used strange phrases with a West Indian lilt. I had to share a desk with another student for a while, and there were a few instances when I was called "four eyes" and one Donald Duck comment, a play on my name that I knew was meant to be funny. These encounters weren't terribly hurtful, but I had never been singled out for ridicule before, and it quieted me. I took solace in my schoolwork and made an effort to impress my teacher.

I chose badly. She was a small, mean woman named Miss Whimby, with a pinched mouth, glasses and one wandering eye. Her thin hair styled in a pageboy, she wore dark skirts and blouses buttoned to the neck with Peter Pan collars. She was punitive and erratic, but I forged on. Trying to show her that I was not just a good student, I appointed myself the teacher's helper. Despite the encroaching darkness, I would stay after school to clean the blackboards and pick up workbooks for her.

No good deed goes unpunished, the saying goes. It certainly applied here, as I discovered the following year, when Miss Whimby was again my teacher. "Show me your work!" she commanded one day, standing at the front of the class. This was a first, so I went up, workbook in hand, a bit anxious about what to do next. To my horror, she became agitated as I turned myself this way and that, holding my workbook so she could see it, when I think I was supposed to just hand it to her.

Suddenly I was on the ground, my glasses skidding across the floor — she had slapped me hard across the face. I was in tears, and there was silence in the room as I scrabbled for my glasses. She sent me off to wash my face, not in the bathroom but in the broom closet nearby. Was she sorry? Did she call my home to explain herself or report what had happened to the principal? She didn't, because she knew I was a weak, frightened child and she guessed that I would do nothing. I was so afraid of getting into trouble that I never told my mother.

I never forgot Miss Whimby's nastiness, and my own servile performance which did nothing to protect me. But that wasn't my only challenge at St. Ignatius. For some reason, the school had installed state-of-the-art washrooms, with a large round communal sink that looked like a fountain and toilets with slightly raised seats that flushed upon impact. Not merely did they flush when you got off them, they flushed when you got on! I was too afraid to show my fear, and as a result never went to the bathroom at school. Walking home in the afternoon, I would have to sit and rock on the low metal pipes that enclosed the little squares of lawn around the apartment buildings, trying to forestall the inevitable, which came as I approached the front door of the apartment. No sooner had I put the key in the door, the urge would come over me and I rarely made it to the toilet without soaking my underpants. I must have covered it up somehow, because once again my mother never knew. I had turned into a child with secrets.

In order for us to have a decent lunch — this was 1960, when kids went home for meals — my mother paid a friend who lived in the apartments on the other side of West Broadway to feed us every day. Barbara had many children and a tall, fair-haired husband, but I recall mostly her daughter Dawn, who was my age. A name with such promise, and she was a composed little girl with a knowing manner, perhaps the result of being a middle child in this bevy of kids. I have no memory of the other siblings or what we ate for lunch; I do remember realizing that they were poor, mainly because the rooms seemed bare of furniture, and even the magical apartment hold-all couldn't disguise the number of people crowded into the space. What made it most clear to me, coming from the tropics where floors were usually polished to a high shine, was looking down at the unpainted wood floors.

I was eleven years old. I could walk to school and back on my own, I had the key to the apartment. But not only was I blocking any feelings of nostalgia for my earlier life, I kept secrets from my mother about what went on at school, and sometimes at home, like my weaponizing a slice of toast and jam against my brother. George and I would fix ourselves snacks after school — Auntie Olga and Uncle Mike had by now moved to Ontario — and one afternoon something he did or said really irritated me. I rarely lashed out, never hit anyone, but I was so incensed that I wanted to teach him a lesson. So I used what was at hand, literally. I flattened the sticky slice on to his face and, as I looked on, not sure whether to be delighted or afraid, George started wailing. "It's in my eyes!" he yelled. "I can't see!" He finally settled down because, unlike the incident in Georgetown, we both realized there was nobody but me to hear him.

So I carried on, not talking about the things that worried me, my daydreams helping me to forget about the bad stuff. I enjoyed our playtime in the school yard, classic skipping games like Double Dutch and a strange practice with a ball in a stocking. I was quite good at these games but not at all ambitious to be the best, mainly because I didn't want to be singled out. I even made friends with a few classmates and felt like I was peering into new worlds when I visited their homes.

Monika was a sweet, quiet girl who wore her long brown hair in two braids. Sometimes she would invite me to her house, which was near the school, before I went home in the afternoon. The 1950s bungalow had metal room dividers between the living and dining rooms and wildly patterned upholstery on the couches. It was permeated by a not unpleasant sour smell, which I later learned was sauerkraut. Monika was the first Polish child I had ever met.

My other friend lived in the apartment complex just behind ours, her balcony also on the first floor. Eleanora was in the grade above me at school, a soft-spoken girl with glossy dark hair, cut just below her ears, and bangs. The youngest sibling in a traditional Italian family, she had the prettiest heart-shaped face, eyes that crinkled when she smiled, and one front tooth that slightly overlapped the other. We would sometimes walk around the neighbourhood, and I recall feeling quite grown up, standing on the sidewalk and chatting with Eleanora as she sat on her balcony.

But mainly, I was alone, my only constant playmate my brother George. I was happy about my new friendships and felt a bit like a Canadian: I could handle cold days, I could encounter people from other cultures. The story of my life had changed, and I wanted to appreciate this new world. So I stifled the longing for sunny days in my grandparents' house with my cousins Roslyn and Janis just beyond the back gate.

Maybe in memory of those days, I took up sleuthing during our time on Upper Lachine Road, just like the Grey Ghosts in those Classics comics. Solo, notebook in hand, I would wander about the neighbourhood looking for some mystery to solve. I remember walking along the sidewalk at Sherbrooke and West Broadway, where a new university building was taking shape — a place where I would eventually teach — jotting down descriptions of building material or of someone standing idly at the corner.

I worked hard at school and tried to fit in. I wasn't too worried about wearing glasses, or even my accent, but now my once curly hair was getting harder to manage and my big front teeth had started to crowd the others in my mouth. I was too young to care about boys, but I began feeling self-conscious. A child at ease with his or her parents might have reached out for solace, but

I couldn't find the words. I could see, as well, that my mother's time was allocated not only to George and myself but to her job and a young Englishman, a friend of one of my uncles, who seemed to be visiting all the time.

I begin to have recurring bad dreams, haunting spectres of dark, faceless creatures who peer at me from around the edges of my bed, poking at my sheets. I can't describe them, even to myself, but they disturb the sheets around my legs somehow and they fill me with anxiety, even dread. I surface into consciousness with my heart beating hard, calling out for my mother. "There's something wrong with my sheets," I wail. "Fix them, fix them." She straightens the sheets, even though she can't see much in the dark.

Sometimes, when I really need calming down, she sits beside me on the bed, her fingers skimming the surface of the warm skin on my back, sending delicious shivers through my body. I love the feeling, the warmth of it reminds me of sitting on Granny's lap or my hand on Grandfather's neck as he drives. The closeness of it feels like home.

I knew that my mother had it in for the church. I later concluded that she never forgave God for my father's death, but at that point all I knew was that she never went to mass. This was a big problem for me, since I also knew that hell awaited people who didn't go to mass on Sunday. But my entreaties that she accompany us could never convince my mother to change her ways. So it came as a big surprise one day when I overheard her saying on the phone, "Yes, Father. Thank you, Father."

"Was that a priest?" I asked jokingly. "What's happening, are you getting married?"

"Yes," she said, and my world fell apart.

A stepfather. I had read "Cinderella," I knew what happened to the girl whose parent marries a stranger. I would be relegated to cleaning the house with a twig broom and doing all the laundry, wearing rags and sleeping behind the stove. I burst into tears, likely not the response my mother had wanted, although I never understood why she didn't think long and hard how to tell her children about this momentous decision. How could she leave it up to chance, especially with her very alert young daughter around? She held me on her lap and still I couldn't stop crying, not until she swore to me, seriously, that I would not end up like Cinderella.

I didn't want a stepfather and was sure I didn't need one. I was too young to articulate this, only I felt it deeply: my brother and I had just been reunited with our mother, but how could she love us when this guy was going to take up all her attention? He was okay, a skinny young man with an English accent, and while I could manage with him around some of the time, for sure I didn't want him there all the time. But as much as my spirit rebelled, I knew my mother would not change her mind.

His name was Bill, and I imagine he must have been quite scared to be inheriting two children, especially when he was such a young man himself — just twenty-five years old. I was in my twenties when I realized with a shock what my mother had done: eleven years after my father had died at the age of twenty-five, she married a man who was twenty-five years old. Funny, sad. For the rest of their lives together, the discrepancy in their ages was kept from us children, and never discussed by those who knew. I was comforted that they died, after nearly sixty happy years together, just two days apart.

But for me, who never acted out, who played the hand I was dealt without much apparent struggle, this marriage was a terrible injury. I was learning grownup ways, and I didn't like them. Grownups acted without realizing what was going on, without seeing the pain they caused their children. Children are resilient, they thought, they'll get over it. But this resilience cost me a lot. I was being forced to accept a father I didn't want, to share a mother I hardly knew.

I remember the feeling of loneliness that pervaded me at the wedding reception at Auntie Thelma's apartment, although I can only recall the details through photographs. In one photo I stand beside my mother, me with cropped hair, big teeth, glasses, she in a beautiful champagne organza shirtwaist dress, an odd lace mantilla on her head. I'm looking up at her, clinging to her arm. In another photo I'm standing against a wall, looking bereft. I never cried after that first great shock, but from that point on, what I had thought of as a cheerful life began to look uncertain and even unhappy.

And it often was. Bill was strict, and as with Miss Whimby, I usually didn't realize that I had transgressed until I was being scolded for something. But over the years, he tried to show that he had value, organizing our family holidays to Prince Edward Island and, my mother would tell me proudly, often picking out my new summer clothing for the vacation. I have a memory of a pleated skort — a short-lived trendy look for the early 1960s: a pair of shorts that resembled a short skirt. I was grudgingly impressed with that sort of thing, but Bill had done even better than that. During our first winter in Canada, he taught us how to skate.

Learning to skate at the age of ten is not easy, and it could be mighty cold out there on the outdoor rink in Montreal West. George, Bill and I walked from the apartment on Upper Lachine Road, leaving the apartment buildings and duplexes for the parkland that housed the skating rink and Montreal West town hall, a part of the neighbourhood with large, single-family houses of two and sometimes three storeys. We would sit on the benches near the rink to put on our skates. I had white figure skates with a bevelled edge at the front; my brother wore brown hockey skates without those edges that could trip you up.

But who cares if he's destined for hockey and I'm not? I'm out there on the ice and I love skating! I have a balaclava that covers my head and keeps my ears warm, and even though it hurts to fall and my nose gets red with cold, I simply love making the blades bite into the ice and keeping my ankles from wobbling in the boots. Then, after what seems like forever, that tentative first shuffle turns into longer and longer glides on the blade. I can begin to concentrate on moving smoothly as I make my way across the ice, and finally, since my current dream is to become a figure skater, I teach myself how to dip into a slow glide on one leg with the other one raised behind me.

So I adapted to this new wintry life with a mother I barely knew but loved without question and a stepfather I accepted but resented. I escaped, reading voraciously and becoming even more immersed in my daydreams. Sometimes, at the dinner table, I was so focused on the story in my head that my loaded fork wouldn't make it into my mouth. This wasn't defiance, though Mum and Bill were constantly reminding me to keep eating.

In any case, mealtime had become boring, at least in the early years when I had to get used to spaghetti or veal cutlets or that dreaded English vegetable, brussels sprouts. Except for occasional visits to Auntie Olga, who might prepare a cook-up rice or spicy chicken curry, our food was Canadian, which in those days meant white bread, frozen vegetables and cuts of meat we never saw in Georgetown. My mother became a good cook, especially after she gave up her secretarial job, but chow mein, metemgee, salt fish stew and delectable pepperpot — no one made them anymore.

Besides, I liked daydreaming. Colourful adventures were filling my head, and I really didn't want to come out. I made up elaborate stories, which were usually versions of those romantic rescues of my childhood with Ros and Janis, this time with flamboyant historical trappings. I was partial to stories with Elizabethan dress and garden paths or to the drapery and courtyards, always featuring stepped bathing ponds, of the Roman period.

Seems to me I had left the garden of my childhood at this point, an unsettling time when I often felt empty and alien, not realizing that there would eventually be a new flowering, another garden. That enduring passage of life that Carl Jung describes, the invisible true life that travels unseen, underground, like a rhizome, only breaking the earth occasionally to flower, didn't feel accessible to me then. "I have never lost a sense of something that lives and endures underneath the external flux," Jung wrote. "What we see is the blossom, which passes. The rhizome remains."

They hadn't been married long when Mum and Bill told us that they had bought a house, and we would be moving to Pointe-Claire, a village and surrounding suburb prettily situated in the western edge of the city on Lake St. Louis, a fluvial lake formed by a widening of the St. Lawrence River. At the time, Lake St. Louis was so polluted that it was known as "Pooey Louie," and children were warned to avoid getting anywhere near the water. In any case, we weren't moving into one of the large ranch homes spread around the lakeshore side of Pointe-Claire.

Our suburban house was located in the newer section above the highway, near a massive new high school and soon-to-be-built hospital. The developers had uprooted trees and cleared fields to build rows of simple homes on gently winding streets, either in two storeys or the ubiquitous 1960s split-level, faced with cut stone. There were roads but the landscaping was unfinished; wooden boards were laid along the muddy front walk. Soon, Mum and Bill had built a path and scattered grass seed, and eventually they created a verdant landscape with flowering trees and bushes.

So I said goodbye to Eleanora, standing on the sidewalk as she sat in a folding chair on her balcony. I tapped my feet, showing off the shoes my mother had just bought for me, in a startling shade of deep olive green, new shoes for a new school. Eleanora and I might have planned to see each other, but in those days twelve-year-olds had no means to do so if their families were not connected. I never saw her again.

Just a few weeks later, in the schoolyard, wearing my new shoes, I was to meet someone who would be a friend for the rest of my life. Patty was freckled, with fair, straight, shoulder-length hair and bangs. Her nose turned up slightly, she had a wide mouth and her front teeth, though as big as mine, weren't crowded in her mouth like mine were. Her eyes were my favourite feature, beautiful green, almond-shaped eyes. She was a fresh-faced, pretty girl, but so very shy that she often put her hand in front of her mouth when she spoke. Was that why she liked me? I was dark, a bit messy, with curly short hair, and even though I was shy inside, outwardly, I might have seemed bold.

She remembers me moving into the group where she was standing, and saying: "I wonder if you can eat lunch here?" It might have been a lame comment, but it got her attention — she thought I was so courageous to speak out in the crowd, she told me years later. And so, our friendship began. Patty was a stranger too, a transplant from Long Island, an Irish American whose dad, an engineer, was part of the team in Montreal to build the city's iconic cruciform skyscraper, Place Ville Marie.

She and I were lucky enough to have landed in this special place, an overflow school that was being used for the Grade 7 classes, situated in the antique, slightly dilapidated village of Pointe-Claire, sharing a small peninsula that reached into the lake with a convent and an ancient church. Unlike the kids at the big Catholic school on the north side of the highway, we were tucked away in this simple building at the end of the road, with views of the lake and old stone buildings.

Another home, another school. I was constantly on alert, often insecure, but there was something magical about the place. I'm not sure why, I can't remember a brogue, but we all knew the school principal was Irish, a good-hearted man with a pale, freckled face and a fondness for singing. We also felt ourselves fortunate to have a beautiful dark-haired gym teacher who, I recall, taught us Israeli folk dances. The school had a small gym but also a running track and green spaces overlooking the lake, where at recess we would call out to the ducks paddling by.

I became very attached to our schoolyard games, especially dodgeball, in which players would congregate on either side of an invisible line and hurl the basketball-sized ball across to hit a player on the opposing team. The element of surprise — which person will the shooter aim for? — changed when the players were whittled down until there might be only two players, then one, on each side. I took to the game with such enthusiasm that I broke the tendon in my middle finger catching the ball and had to wear a cast for about a month. That was the bad news; the good news was that I stopped biting my fingernails, a habit I had throughout childhood.

To my surprise, I was chosen to "show" the other kids how to run — who knew I had a good running stride? — in preparation for a city-wide track and field meet. I should have been happy, but I was pre-adolescent. My strongest memory of the daylong event was my humiliation: because the girls had to wear shorts and white blouses, everyone would see that I was still in an undershirt. I had tried mental telepathy in an effort to nudge my mother to buy me a bra; my process was to say each day, when she returned from work, "Did you buy me anything today?" "No," she would answer, with a puzzled look. Despite the sunny day and the excitement of the event, my embarrassment was so acute that I couldn't concentrate at all on the competition. My graceful stride brought me no medals.

There was another school competition at which I fared better, however: getting good grades. There were two classroom teachers, a messy-looking red-haired woman and the one I was lucky enough to get, a tall man with a moustache and slicked back dark hair. Mr. P was kind and encouraging to me, maybe because I was such an attentive student. I had kept up my studious behaviour — I can recall Saturday afternoons when George and Bill watched the football game on TV while I sat at my bedroom desk doing homework.

Occasionally I managed to come first in class, besting a clever, talkative boy named Gordon. We weren't competitive types, at least I never felt that way, although he was a smart, sometimes sassy character, so articulate that everyone in class realized how much he knew. I was the quiet, hard-working type. I certainly preferred being at the top of the class; I needed the feeling of value that came with it. But what really mattered to me, I learned in Grade 7, was writing. To my wonder and delight, the teacher marked one of my compositions, something about birds and clouds, by saying that he had never given out an A before, but he found such beautiful, descriptive writing in my composition that he had to do so this time. I had been reading, ingesting words since I was a young child, but my love affair with using words began at that moment.

Patty and I spent countless hours together. I learned about American habits like having sweet rolls at breakfast, and I always felt welcomed by the good cheer that pervaded her house. Her father was one of the funniest grownups I had ever met. She was an only child, but hers was a Canadian version of my tropical life — she lived next door to an aunt, uncle and three cousins who were constantly dropping in. Sometimes we would go to my house after school, and since my mother was in the city at her secretarial job, we blissed out on buttered toast sprinkled with cinnamon and sugar. I would take my orange-and-white portable record player to the basement where we would play 45s, swaying and hugging ourselves as though we were each dancing in the arms of a special boy.

In the early morning before school, I would occasionally visit that beautiful grey stone church, the sun glittering on the lake and seagulls calling, to pray for my mother to start attending mass on Sundays. And I remember clearly the day, on my morning visit to church, that I found myself kneeling with tightly clasped hands, facing the marble altar and the tall wooden cross on which Jesus hung, praying for a certain cute, dark-haired boy at school to notice me. Neither prayer was answered.

At home in Pointe-Claire, having a stepfather continued to be a mostly bitter pill. I did appreciate the cheery yellow and white scalloped wallpaper that Bill put up in my room and the fitted white furniture with dressing table, desk and bureau neatly lining one wall. I only realized in retrospect that he coped with being overwhelmed by this instant family of two growing children by doing his best to feel that he was in control. So in addition to a pretty restrictive bedtime, he instituted weird rules that were nothing like I remembered from my grandparents' home.

For instance, a teenage girl needs to look extra good at school. Even though for the first few years, the boys and girls took separate classes at my Catholic high school, we still saw each other in the cafeteria. So it made perfect sense to me that, like all my school friends, I would put my hair in curlers each night, especially since my curly hair was by then morphing into wavy hair, which is a lot harder to handle. Not to Bill. He got it into his head that curlers were unhealthy for the scalp, and so they were banned. Convinced that I was the only high school girl not allowed to curl her hair, I came up with a West Indian solution: strips of toilet paper and bobby pins. Every night I folded locks of hair inside a piece of toilet paper, rolled it around and pinned it to my scalp.

Bill also insisted that I was too young to attend school dances during the first year of high school, a decision that made no sense to me. Why would a school have dances if the students were too young to go? I felt noticeable by my absence, a difficult situation for someone who just wanted to be part of the group. Nothing feeds rebellion like rules and strictures, and that's where this was heading.

Maybe because Bill was a reserved Brit who couldn't figure me out, or because I didn't know how to behave without the constant, easy closeness that I had in the tropics, I never managed to feel warmth toward him until much later in life. I realize now that he had been out of his depth in his new family, and that his own childhood story was complicated: he was evacuated to the British countryside during the Second World War, complete with cardboard suitcase and gas mask, and did not return to his home in East London for five years. He admitted that he had liked it in the countryside. Did he think that I would also be happy to give up my extended family and the only home I had known? He seemed blind to how much I was hurting.

Poor guy. He had found the woman he loved and continued to love throughout their long life together, but I didn't make it easy. He took the right approach with George: they bonded over cars and sports. But even though I was an insecure kid who wanted to please, his controlling behaviour infuriated me. Our regular confrontations might have been easy to dismiss in a family where parental love was taken for granted, but these arguments chipped away at my relationship with my mother. In her telling, she pushed back only once on his strictness; most of the time she opted to put up a united front. "Exactly the wrong approach" was my thinking, as I transitioned from obedient, cheery, straight-A student to surly, difficult teenager.

I never rebelled in a major way; no drug taking or promiscuity, although I learned how to smoke cigarettes by sneaking Bill's du Mauriers, which he kept in a dresser drawer. They tasted horrible, and I think I turned green the first few times I inhaled. But smoking was an element of cool, and I had given up caring about good grades to pursue being one of the group, so I persisted. Some of my ventures had results that I didn't anticipate, like the "beatnik" party I decided to throw in our Pointe-Claire house.

I had decorated the family room, and everyone was supposed to come looking like a beatnik — remember, it was still the early

1960s. The party unravelled quickly: first, the friends who turned up insisted on turning out the lights while we danced. Then Mum and Bill decided to check out the scene and came downstairs just as one of my girlfriends, the one who arrived in see-through black tights, was in full view, necking with the boy she liked. On went the lights and there stood my parents, horrified, especially seeing one of my close friends being so "brazen." The party soon lost its lustre in the brightly lit room and as the guests trickled out, I felt relieved but mostly embarrassed, both that the party had spiralled out of control and that I had been exposed as being not at all cool.

There was a constant push and pull, mostly about control, and I remember vowing, after one particularly tumultuous argument as I drowned my sorrows in the shower, steam and sadness rising around me, that I would never, ever spend more years with these people than I had lived with my grandparents in South America. I wouldn't give them the satisfaction, I thought. It turned out that, even though I no longer felt the need to make the point, I was true to my word. I left home at the age of eighteen, just eight years after my ten-year-old self had arrived in Canada.

What that meant to my mother, I never knew. The years George and I were with her, from pre-adolescence into adolescence, are hard years for any parent to navigate, and only when I was an adult did our relationship become easier. But in quieter, less resentful times, rare at that point, I would remember all that I had lost. It could be so simple, like a soft summer breeze or a West Indian accent. Or it could be powerful, like hearing someone address their father as Daddy. "Daddy," I thought, "Daddy." I have never in my life called anyone Daddy.

As my West Indian accent faded, I slowly began to feel comfortable in this place where I lived. I managed at school. I had friends. It might be possible now, I thought, to pass for a regular Canadian. I didn't look different from anyone else, a young white female like so many people in the city, province, country. But here in Quebec we were strangers in another way, speaking English with our Caribbean accents amid a population of French speakers. Many of my relatives who started out in Montreal eventually became part of the Guyanese diaspora around Toronto.

Like Bob Dylan, whose songs I didn't understand but listened to with increasing fascination, I pitied the poor immigrant, myself, who wishes she could have stayed home. Because I really wasn't at home. Mum and Bill cared for us, and I was pretty sure that I could depend on them, but I had gone from being a parentless child in a cherished country to a parented child in a country where I had no story. I was the immigrant who looked like she fitted in — but really, she had never wanted to leave home.

More than anything, I felt myself an invisible observer, standing apart from everyone else. In South America, the place that formed me and circumscribed my life, I resembled a child of privilege even though I was missing the crucial support of parental love. In Montreal, although I passed easily for a standard English Canadian once my accent was gone, I felt different on a deep, unexplainable level.

People would ask me, "You come from where?" I was a stranger to this country, posing as a Canadian child. And there was no home to go back to, to paraphrase Thomas Wolfe. British Guiana gained independence and became Guyana, and the majority Black and Indian population became the stakeholders of the country — which made perfect sense. My Portuguese ancestry was reduced to a footnote.

And another conundrum. As I grew older and began to feel more at ease in my Canadian skin, especially going to university and sharing apartments with Canadian friends, I started to feel less connected to my own past, my tropical story. I still loved to be around when the relatives gathered and the stories about home were told, fables enhanced, adventures colourized; in fact, I felt even hungrier for reminiscences of home. But something changed inside me.

Even though I am recognizable to everyone as Donna, I feel separate, disengaged. I see myself at the only family reunion ever held for this growing Gomes brood, aunts and uncles joining with cousins — I eventually count forty cousins from the Portuguese side. We are a large, lively crowd, and it's a sunny summer day on the expansive grounds of my parents' home in the Ontario countryside. My mother and my brother George lounge under the spreading oak tree, surrounded by a few of the younger cousins. Auntie Edna is working in the kitchen, turning out delectable flaky rotis on the griddle, while my cousin Paul wanders through the clusters of people with his movie camera, stopping to joke with his siblings, Roslyn and Janis. By the pool, Uncles Steve, Stanley and Frank are chatting with their sisters Lucille and Olga whose husbands, the uncles I spent so much time with during my Guyanese childhood, stand near Bill at the barbecue, beers in hand, Brits comfortable around each other. Meanwhile, the cousins' children, their numbers increasing annually, are splashing about in the swimming pool situated just beyond the house before the land falls away into paddocks and fields.

I'm happy, I feel good to be here, watching and listening. These relatives congregate, talk about home, still with their singsong West Indian accents. But something has changed. I'm a Canadian now, a young feminist, I read poetry and attend university. My accent is gone.

They're getting married, having children, hanging out together; some of them are still practising Catholics. I'm a decade away from marriage and kids, I have friends with radical ideas, I go to marches protesting the war in Vietnam and nuclear testing. I have no time for Catholicism. I want to learn what's really going on in the world, to stand up for human rights, and there in the literature I have begun to understand the damage wrought by colonialism. Life was not as beautiful as it seemed in my tropical garden.

chapter 8

finding the words

Putting words to an experience of loss is considered a sure way to explore and understand it. "People who lose their childhood eventually have to retrieve it," Michael Ondaatje wrote. Sometimes loss, though, especially in those early years, has no words. My search felt more like a vague sadness, a subtle yearning. I didn't know what I was looking for until it found me.

At first, it was the phrases in songs that moved me, the ability of a lyric to find the centre of a feeling — just like the Platters did in my childhood. By my early teens, even though I was swept up by the phenomenon of the early 1960s girl groups with their great melodies and mundane lyrics, the songs I loved were the ones that expressed longing. I listened over and over to Peter, Paul and Mary's bittersweet song "Whatshername," the secret search for a lost love, and to Gordon Lightfoot's haunting melodies about being far away from home and missing his loved one. Nana Mouskouri was a sensation at the time and I couldn't get enough of her plaintive version of "Un Canadian Errant." I connected with her words about longing for her unhappy country, and with Leonard Cohen's remembered goodbyes and eyes soft with sorrow.

We had no classical music culture in our home in Pointe-Claire; Bill was a jazz fan and my mother became one too. I, on the other hand, spent hours playing Claude Debussy's *Clair de lune*; Erik Satie's evocative *Gymnopédies* felt to me like wistful yearning for the past and the future. I didn't share this with my friends; just me and my record player in my yellow and white bedroom, the window overlooking my parents' carefully tended garden, and the rows and rows of streets and houses clustered around the massive high school needed to educate all those baby boomers.

Then I began to search for expression in poetry, even the classics we had to memorize in my early grades. I loved most of them, but the poem that showed me what words could do was Alfred Noyes' "The Highwayman." The fast pace, the daring escapades, the love, the loss. It was all there, and how he used words!

> The wind was a torrent of darkness among the gusty trees.
> The moon was a ghostly galleon tossed upon cloudy seas.
> The road was a ribbon of moonlight over the purple moor,
> And the highwayman came riding—
> Riding—riding—
> The highwayman came riding, up to the old inn-door.

By the time I was in Grade 12 at Montreal High School, I had transitioned to low-key hippie and it felt good, although I had no plans for a future, no real connection with my past. Then, in English class, I was jolted out of my torpor when the teacher read from T.S. Eliot's epic poem *The Waste Land,* something about the month of April being particularly cruel because this is when the spring rains begin to soften the hard ground, awakening thoughts of the past and even glimpses of the future. I remembered that afternoon nap with Grandfather and the melancholy and hope that floated toward me through the open windows of my home in Georgetown. So when Eliot wrote about memory and desire, I didn't understand it, but I knew it. His earlier poem "The Love Song of J. Alfred Prufrock," about the sad man glimpsing the lives of others, in which he paints a picture of darkening streets and lonely men leaning out of windows, remains the clearest evocation of longing I have ever read. I devoured as much poetry as I could fit into my life, e e cummings and Anne Sexton, Yevgeny Yevtushenko and Edna St. Vincent Millay, everything by Leonard Cohen and Margaret Atwood, loving it all and understanding little, casting for the tidbits that spoke to me. Then, much later, I discovered the nuanced eloquence of Seamus Heaney, whose poetry about writing I often shared with journalism students. How well the great Irish poet conveyed loss and the meaning of family, nowhere better than in "Clearances," his heartbreaking remembrance of his mother, centred on the mundane task of peeling potatoes together:

So while the parish priest at her bedside
Went hammer and tongs at the prayers for the dying
And some were responding and some crying
I remembered her head bent towards my head,
Her breath in mine, our fluent dipping knives –
Never closer the whole rest of our lives.

◇

Canada is an easy place to call home, a benevolent, mild-mannered country. And after a few years, I learn to identify as Canadian just like the millions of other immigrants who become citizens — although among my friends and colleagues as I grow older, I am often the only first-generation immigrant. I realize the usefulness of being Canadian when I travel to Europe at the age of eighteen and am forced to use a passport from Trinidad and Tobago, where I was born, my British passport no longer valid after British Guiana's independence.

Customs officials don't know what to make of this young white woman with a pretty blue passport from a Caribbean island, and I get plenty of raised eyebrows. These looks might also have something to do with my newly acquired hippie dress of worn bell-bottoms, scarves and beads. Ironically, it is only travelling into Belgium, the country I believed my father's family came from, where I am taken into a windowless room and interrogated.

When people emigrate from other countries, they say they come from Latvia or China, or they're from England or France, Peru or New Zealand. Rarely do they come from a country whose very name is so associated with colonialism that it is no longer used. So when British Guiana became Guyana, another piece of my history fell away. When I say I'm half Portuguese, then I have to explain that I'm not from Portugal, no, but from Madeira, an island settled by Portugal, but we left there for a country that was once owned by Britain but isn't any more.

Yet I fit into this country of immigrants, no different from many Canadians in saying that the place of my childhood exists only in my memory. And I can argue that this self-described role as observer, as the one who notices the game in progress but rarely feels an active participant, is part of the definition of being a journalist. Who better than an unencumbered voyager to see and describe the way things are?

But, as I've learned, there is no such thing as an unencumbered voyager.

Perhaps my growing commitment to the practice of yoga, my search for a deeper awareness, aren't just symptoms of my status as an aging baby boomer. Perhaps I'm finally on the path of understanding where all this sunshine and sadness are leading me. "When the ego weeps for what it has lost, the spirit rejoices for what it has found," goes a Sufi saying.

My parents played a huge part in this. Not only did their passing lead me to become more invested in yoga and meditation, their last years softened my attitude. Their dreaded diagnoses — Mum with Alzheimer's and Bill, a year or so later, with Lewy body dementia — offered me an unexpected gift. Over the four or five years of their decline, I finally acquired the role of dutiful daughter, visiting regularly, taking them on outings, escorting her to the hairdresser, walking him to the bank.

As I grew older, I had begun to admire Bill's view of the world. A curious, careful man, he seemed to enjoy everything that came his way, from chatting with the butcher or handyman to that busy commute into Toronto and back. He was methodical, thoroughly engaged in his business life as an expert in reinsurance, and in his personal interests like jam-making or reading. I can remember, after we had all left the table at Christmas or Thanksgiving, that he would take the turkey into the kitchen and completely strip the bird, separating white and dark meat on two platters, and then start the stock with the carcass. It could take hours.

I discovered that Bill was one of those business executives beloved by the steakhouses of Chicago and New York. He enjoyed martinis and New York sirloin, and anything with garlic. There he is before dinner, in a soft plaid shirt and corduroys, sitting on the wide wraparound porch of my parents' red-brick Victorian home in the Ontario countryside with his paperback novel, something by Len Deighton or John le Carré, sipping from a glass of Scotch, neat. I appreciate him, finally.

My mother, in these last years, showed a childish sweetness despite the confusion of her dementia. The mute disdain that I had felt for so long, holding her at arm's length, disappeared.

I had always felt that she showed her emotions too easily, even though I recognized she could have startling flashes of deep wisdom. And I considered her much too dependent on Bill and my brother, less and less able over time to articulate her own needs. No question that Bill was devoted to her, or that George was generous and caring, but where was her independence, I wondered. Finally I came to see that, after the tragedy of her younger life, she wished more than anything to feel protected. She got what she needed here. How could I criticize that?

She knew it was coming. Even before the dementia diagnosis, we went to dinner one night and she drank several Scotches and confessed that something sinister was happening to her memory. "It's normal to forget things, Ma," I said to her. But she was right; we got the picture after a test that humiliated her with questions she couldn't answer. She started to repeat herself, would stare for hours at a single page of the morning paper, and could be stubborn and wilful. "No, I'm not going to the dentist, I'm not going!" she declared the morning I arrived at the door of their apartment in the seniors' residence in Ottawa. I had left Montreal at six a.m. to take them to their appointment. No amount of cajoling would change her mind.

She never stopped loving walks in the country, where I would drive them sometimes, and would always exclaim about the wildflowers at the side of the road. She loved sparkles, so when I visited I took to wearing sparkly skirts or earrings, which she never failed to notice. We marked her ninety-second birthday with a gathering in the party room, and my mother, pretty in a green linen shirt with blush on her cheeks, her lovely white hair nicely cut, blew out the candles on her little cake, the pink icing dotted with rose petals. She shone, sitting beside Bill on the small settee. Four months later, they were both gone. I would recall the day of her party as I ventured on a six a.m. beach walk in the Bahamas a few months after they died. As I turned to look up at the sky lightening behind me, I saw the fading moon and beside it, a twinkling star. "There they are," I thought, "Mum and Bill together."

After she died, I found in her dresser drawer a small notebook made of hand-pressed paper that I had brought her from a trip to South Africa, when I was working on a book about activist women around the world. My mother had attended a launch event in Toronto where I spoke about the book, and afterward looked at me with shining eyes. "I'm so proud of you," she said, almost shyly. There was no writing in this notebook except on one page where I found, in my mother's hand, the words of the eighteenth-century poet Thomas Campbell: "To live in hearts we leave behind is not to die."

It struck me as so prescient, so telling of this journey, as I try to bring into the light some of the stories and mysteries of her life. I had the words inscribed on her headstone, trimmed with a carving of oak leaves to represent the countryside she loved more and more as she aged. The stone, which she shares with my stepfather, is a memento mori but also an example of the confusion I felt when it came to naming her. I tried to pay homage to everyone in her life and ended up with GWEN (NEBENZAHL) HOLBROOK née GOMES. I just needed it to be there, all of it.

I don't remember when I understood that by growing up without a mother and father I was not like everyone else. How could I sort out the feelings that a child is expected to have about their mum and dad, the reciprocity of love and devotion they're meant to feel?

What did those early sunshine years give me, in that country I remember so well, vivid yet forever lost? I've thought many times about going back to visit, and I'm encouraged by the push underway in Guyana to carve out a place for itself as an eco-conscious destination, though leery about its discovery of massive oil deposits, troubling as our climate crisis deepens. But I can't bring myself to see my grandparents' home in its new guise as a government building, even though I'm stunned to discover that it also houses the Honorary Consulate of Trinidad and Tobago. It's as though my story is still lodged there.

"It doesn't have the tower anymore," Auntie Olga exclaimed, "and the room under the house is gone!" But it doesn't matter about the physical place, because I believe I've found a new home for my family in these memories and historical records. Mary Fowke, a psychotherapist and author, says that the act of writing memoir is its own form of dwelling or abode-making.

My memory, however fallible, lives in the writing. This is where I've created my own "home of words."

It has taken a lot of time and thought to reach the place in my psyche where my father resides, if such a thing is even possible. The moment of absorbing the meaning of his death was a great leap forward; before that he was just a vague character, a shadow without shape or discernible features. Then, a year after my mother died, while staying in a yoga ashram, I attended a workshop on visualization and for the first time "saw" my father not as a frozen image in a black and white photo but as a live human being, in khaki pants and short-sleeved white shirt, walking toward me, reaching for my hand. He was handsome, just as he was in those photos, and he was present for me. A door had opened in my imagination, and how happy I felt, yet profoundly sad that this was the only way I could find him.

In a talk about compassion, the gentle, wise Buddhist teacher Thich Nhat Hanh encourages us to do this meditation for a few weeks: revisit our own self as a five-year-old. "Look at that child, and smile at that child," he says. "Show that child love and compassion." I visualize myself as a little girl, standing by the front gate of my grandparents' home.

Then he offers this deep insight: "Now imagine your own father as a five-year-old boy. Five years old, a child is very vulnerable, easily hurt. Smile with compassion upon your father."

This meditation connects the two of us, and it's revelatory. My father is five years old, around the age he would have been when he arrived in Georgetown. Fronds of tall palm trees sway in the warm breeze. I smile at his five-year-old self, the one I know in those photographs, with the level gaze, the hazel eyes. The sun is streaming and I'm here too, five years old, a curly-haired, brown-eyed girl in this magical, tropical land.

I look at him with compassion; he smiles back at me. We are connected, innocent children starting our lives.

acknowledgments

I am forever indebted to my Portuguese grandparents as well as my aunts Olga and Lucille, my cousins Ros and Janis and all my Madeiran family, who provided me with such comfort during those early years in South America. I offer one hand in thanks while in the other I'm carrying an olive branch, because while they have been the subject of so much of this writing, there's a good chance that not all our memories line up. Growing up so close to my brother George, I know I've taken his childhood experiences for granted. We were together during those formative years, and I'm grateful for his company.

That said, I've done my very best to record the past as clearly as I could. Most of that Guyanese generation are no longer with us, but I hope they would approve. My mother and stepfather were faced with a little girl who struggled to navigate the loss of one childhood and the difficult flowering of another. I thank them for their patience and quiet support, and the example they set as two people determined to make the best of every day.

To my Nebenzahl family, I'm so grateful to my Aunt Gloria for keeping me connected, at some expense to herself. In that part of the book, archival research took me on a journey I never anticipated, one that has allowed me to peer into a shadowy past. For help with that, I must thank researcher Jackie Schwartz from Antwerp, who offered me the benefit of her investigative skills. Jackie was instrumental in uncovering the story of my paternal grandparents and the fate of my grandfather Joseph Nebenzahl. The archival resources at the Shoah Memorial, Yad Vashem and the Paris Archives also helped me reconstruct the ultimately harrowing details of his life.

Searching for background on Georgetown and British Guiana, I was inspired by British writer Margaret Bacon's first book, *Journey to Guyana*, as well as V.S. Naipaul's *The Middle Passage*. I am very thankful for the writing of Guyanese scholar Sister Mary Noel Menezes and her book *The Portuguese of Guyana: A Study in Culture and Conflict.*

I was lucky enough to meet, on a ferry in Nova Scotia, Lisbon-based Canadian psychotherapist and author Mary Fowke, whose PhD thesis on the language of displacement in memoir helped me understand the power of words in recreating the past. I was bowled over when she casually described her subject: the memoirs of three writers who had come to Canada when they were young. Mary's insight and her commentary on the manuscript added important layers to my understanding of my own journey.

My interest in retrieving the past, dormant for decades, was stimulated by the work of author Natalie Goldberg, an enthusiastic teacher who links writing memoir with the practice of Zen Buddhism. Her book *Writing Down the Bones* helped open doors in my memory and was a catalyst for the writing exercises that I developed and shared with friends during the months I spent at an ashram in the Bahamas several years ago. I was also inspired, as I laboured to describe old photos, by the ability of American documentary filmmaker Ken Burns to linger over the grainy photographs of soldiers and their families in his TV series on the American Civil War.

I have been encouraged every step of the way by former newspaper colleague turned nonfiction writer and poet Mark Abley. I showed Mark my early writing and can still recall the stirrings of hope I felt when he said those important words: "This could be a book." He pointed me in the direction of Stonehewer Books in B.C. and I'm doubly fortunate that he has added the title of book editor to his long list of credentials. At Stonehewer Books, publisher George Galt's keen insights were instrumental in shaping the story. I thank him and managing editor Ned Seager for their guidance and expertise.

My first reader and greatest supporter was and is my husband, Mark Swift. Not only did he nudge me over the years to keep writing, but he fuelled me with toast and coffee delivered to my writing space on the second floor of our island cottage in Nova Scotia. Big Tancook Island, with its cool breezes and changing weather, was a welcome backdrop to my early scribbling and my later, more concerted efforts to meet a publisher's deadline.

I thank all the friends who encouraged me, and especially those who were generous enough to read the early manuscript or offer expertise on the visuals I've used in the book. And while it might seem strange to acknowledge yoga as an inspiration, in the ten years since I've been (mostly) committed to this contemplative practice, I have been strengthened and renewed by its combination of physical discipline and spiritual insights.

And finally, the wonder of it all, I'm grateful to my children Katrina and Devin, who have without knowing it been my guiding stars. To have played a part in ushering in the next generation has been my greatest reward. This is their story, too.

about the author

Donna Nebenzahl left British Guiana — now known as Guyana — at the age of 10 and grew up in Montreal. She studied at McGill University and has been a reporter and editor at several major Canadian dailies as well as a freelance magazine writer. She is an adjunct professor of journalism at Concordia University, and the author of *Womankind: Faces of Change Around the World*. She conceived and wrote a documentary film about Elsie Reford, *Twice Upon a Garden*, as well as the environmental blog Earthbound. She and her husband live in Montreal and Big Tancook Island, Nova Scotia.

credits

Excerpts from "Four Quartets" by T.S. Eliot appear courtesy of Faber and Faber Ltd.

Excerpt from *Memories, Dreams, Reflections* by Carl Jung appears courtesy of Penguin Random House.

Seamus Heaney's "Clearances," from *Death of a Naturalist*, appears courtesy of Faber and Faber Ltd.

"My Prayer" performance lyrics by The Platters® All rights reserved 2025 with permission by Frederick J. Balboni, Jr., Herb Reed Enterprises, LLC.

Excerpts from Mary Noel Menezes, *The Portuguese of Guyana: A Study in Culture and Conflict* (London: M. N. Menezes, 1994) used with permission.

The Michael Ondaatje quotation on page 188 is from a lecture the author gave called "Mongrel Art" at the Santa Maddalena Foundation on June 13, 2012.

The Michael Ondaatje quotation on page 221 is from "Michael Ondaatje: The Divided Man." *The Guardian*, 18 August 2011.

The Pema Chödrön quotation is from *When Things Fall Apart: Heart Advice for Difficult Times* and appears courtesy of Shambhala Publications.

The photograph of a deportation document on page 176 is courtesy of the Memorial de la Shoah, Paris, France.

Back cover photo: The author outside the family home in Georgetown with her cousin Janis, in the early 1950s.